THE

JOURNEY BACK

TO NOW

Robert C. Sherrill

Printed in the United States of America

First Printing, 2018

ISBN: 0-9998759-0-6

RCS Publishing

475 Metroplex Drive, Suite 503

Nashville, TN 37211

www.robertcsherrill.com

Dedication

This book is dedicated to my babies. Daddy loves you all and you are the reason why I push everyday to become better than the man I was yesterday. Remember that life's journey is what you make it and to always have each other's backs no matter what. I am your loudest cheerleader and your strongest crutch. I hope that you all are as proud of me as I am of each of you.

Contents

Acknowledgments

I would like to acknowledge the women in my family who played a critical role in my upbringing...my grandmother Hattie Fletcher who always had positive things to say about her RobRob and loved me regardless of my shortcomings, my aunt Charlene McClain who made sure I kept God as the head of my life, my mother Freda Sherrill who makes me a proud son and who I love dearly, my cousin Deborah White and my aunt Margaret White who took me in when no one else would. To my aunt Charlene McClain, grandmother Hattie Fletcher and dad, Robert Batey, I know you all are smiling down on me and I can only pray that I am making you proud. You left me far too soon and I think of you often. To my uncle John Sherrill, thank you for always being there for me. To my sister Tiffany and my brother Frederick, you both are my troopers and I know that when the odds are stacked against me, I can count on you to have my back. To my children, you each saved me and push me to be the best man and father that I could ever possibly be. I'm not perfect, but I promise you that the love I have for each of you is.

Foreword

Hello, I am Robert's mom and he asked me to write a letter to put in his book about his life and addictions. We both have been through a lot during the course of life, and we both are truly blessed to still be here by the grace of God!! Whoever reads this book, we are blessed, and we hope and pray that it will give you the hope and understanding in your journey through life's ups and downs. Well I was a drug addict for 20 years and I fought that battle for a long time in the process, but I have come to find out that that's what that drug cocaine does to you. You don't mean to hurt the ones you love, but it's the insanity and the disease of it that nobody ever explains to you. You just think that you are crazy, but you are NOT! I got started when I was a young single mother of 2 at the time, and I had a lot of things going on with so much responsibility on me with no help in sight! I was all on my own. Nobody ever understood me or even tried!!

My son asked me what was my "turnaround" point and I told him it was when I felt like I was about to die. I called my daughter and told her that I wouldn't be here when she woke up the next morning. At that time, I was living with her trying to get clean. She was grown by then, so she said mom don't talk like that when you get up in the morning, just go to the doctor and find out what's wrong. I didn't have any more strength to fight and was willing to just lay there and die because I felt death at that moment. But thanks to my Father in Heaven, He wasn't done with me yet so He woke me up the next morning and I headed to the hospital. They told me to come back the next day but it would have been too late. On my way back home a lady ran the red light and struck my car. I hit my head on my daughter's steering wheel. The ambulance came. The officer said that I needed to go to the hospital because there was a cut over my eye. It wasn't bleeding, but you could see the white meat. I told the officer I felt ok enough to go to my daughter's home which was a street over and I will get her to take to the hospital because I didn't have insurance. They allowed me to leave and my family took me to the hospital. My wound was still not bleeding but it was open. The doctors came in and were in awe that I was still living and talking! They couldn't get any blood from me anywhere, so they rushed me upstairs for a blood transfusion because they said I shouldn't be living right now it was of course a miracle from God. Because it wasn't my time to go yet, God was not finished with me. He still had things for me to do. When I was able to leave the hospital, I was so happy and so grateful that my Father not only saved me from the desires of drugs, but from the stronghold of death. He also gave me life and forgave me of all my sins like He always does, because He loves us no matter what...because that's what He does. He is our Creator and our Father, and He loves us even when we don't know how to love ourselves.

As of February 4, 2018, I have been blessed with 14 years clean, and God has kept His promises to me (all of them). I have a wonderful husband and a great job, a great home and a peaceful place in my heart and head—thanks be to my Father (God)!

If you only knew how much God loves and cares for us, then you will eventually turn everything over to Him lock, stock and barrel. I promise you, if He did it for me He will do it for you too! He gives his toughest battles to some of his strongest soldiers and I am thankful that my son is using the darkness of his past to light the way for the youth in this city.

To God Be the Glory,

Signed Robert's Mom

CHAPTER 1

Stolen Innocence

They say our first memories as a child start to fade around age seven. We get some type of amnesia that erases the bliss and freedom found in innocence before we really start to deal with the unfiltered environment that surrounds us. Your childhood has always been thought to be the greatest days of your life. Your biggest concern was what game to play. The biggest decisions were made by eenie, meenie, miney, mo, and the only true crime was not making it home before the streetlights came on. While some could look back on their childhood with a longing for the days that once were, there were some of us that truly had

> **"There were some of us that truly had to embrace the reality of the hardships and struggle that was, recognize how it shaped what is, and use it as motivation for what would be.**

to embrace the reality of the hardships and struggle that was, recognize how it shaped what is, and use it as motivation for what would be.

Bits and pieces of my childhood were lost, but I did remember some of the impactful moments that related to the journey back to now. I started out a regular kid with no cares or worries in the world. It was my older sister, myself, and the man I thought was my biological father at the time. We stayed on 10th Avenue N. in Nashville, and we lived a normal life. I did the typical things: go outside and play, ride my bike, enjoy family outings. But that's all I remembered, until the argument that my mother and father had. To this day, I didn't truly know how I knew what was happening, but I did. I pulled my father outside and asked, with a face full of tears, if they were going to get a divorce. He wiped my tears and reassured me that they wouldn't be getting a divorce. Even in his comfort, I still had a fear that something was going to happen. Intuition? Reasoning? Recognition of issues? I didn't know what it was, but it proved to be right. The next thing I knew, we were moving to Nashville's infamous "Dodge City" housing projects. It was a two-bedroom apartment, but we didn't have a lot of material possessions. My grandmother gave us beds, and we took up trying to make our

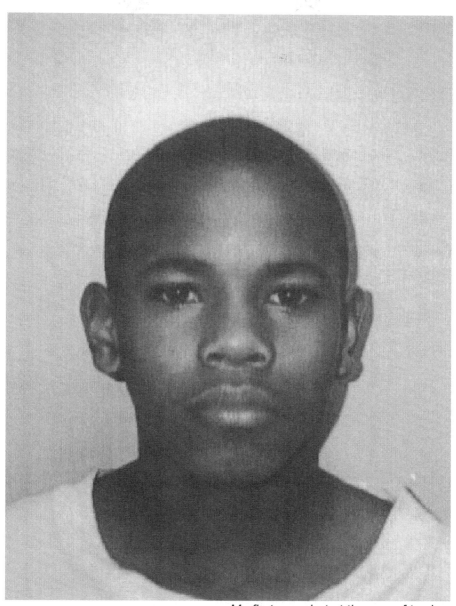

My first mugshot at the age of twelve.

house a home. My mom used to instill in us that 'we were all we got' and that family meant everything.

At first, everything was normal. Our first day of school, we got on the bus on the way back home. Being the 'new kids,' we forgot to get off at the bus stop. My sister grabbed my hand and told me we had to walk to our grandmother's house because that was the only place we knew to go. Little did we know, our mom was at the bus stop waiting on us. When my mom finally thought to look for us at my grandmother's house, I remember her walking in and being so relieved that we were okay. From that moment on, we were to get off the bus at a neighbor's house and wait on my mother there.

> **"Life was normal, but then, like everything, there was a change.**

Life was normal, but then like, everything, there was a change. It was the type of change that shattered every sense of stability and normalcy around you. At this point, crack was becoming the newest trend and the biggest devastation to the community. The addictions and behaviors rooted in the drug had torn many families apart and left in its wake many broken pieces. My family was one of its casualties.

It didn't happen suddenly; its attack was subtle.

There were trivial things like the first of the month coming and the food not being replenished to last throughout the month, or the toiletries and household care items being absent. We would have to use newspaper for toilet paper, having to ball it up and rub it together to make it soft. We used baking soda for toothpaste and deodorant if we didn't have any store-bought toiletries around. Our tub became the washing machine, and the stove became the dryer. I ruined a lot of pants falling asleep during the dry cycle, and they would burn. Meals went from a meat and three, to bologna sandwiches, sugar bread, ketchup and cheese sandwiches, ramen noodles, and mayo sandwiches. We used to go to the WIC office and get the big block of government cheese, which was debatably some of the best cheese ever.

As young as I was, I knew something was wrong and so did my sister. Much like the intuition that led me to the divorce conversation with my father, I had a moment that opened my eyes to what was happening. My sister and I would sit and talk about how to find out what was really going on. The plan was to start searching the house. A few days later, we found what we were looking for. In the bathroom, near the ceiling, there was a *sweet spot* that could go unnoticed... but, of course, I was nosy and found her hiding spot. I didn't know what exactly it was, but I knew that if it was hidden, it had to be bad. What I found, I now knew to be a crack pipe. It was a mini plastic liquor bottle (nips) with a three-inch antenna stuck through a hole in its side. Remember, this was when crack first hit, so people were *resourceful*, for lack of a better word.

I showed my sister my findings, and we confronted my mother. She snatched it back and asked why we were 'meddling.' Instead of backing down, we stood our ground and asked what it was. We were so angry and confused that all we wanted were answers. My mom cried and promised better days. Being a child, I went to bed hopeful, equipped with the promises she made. Things only got worse.

For weeks and months after that, we were still finding paraphernalia. She was still hiding it, but we were still searching because the promises went unfulfilled. If it wasn't for my aunt who lived next door, there would have been many times we didn't eat. Although there were dark times, having someone close who cared offered a sliver of hope, stability, and fun. I remember the first time I saw crack.

At this point, we were just going off the paraphernalia that we would find. We had never seen my mom use the drug—and that was something that I could still say to this day. I walked in the house and it was dark. I opened doors to all the rooms, and my mom was in my room passed out with crack cocaine spilled all over the bed. I made sure she was breathing and picked up the crack rocks and hid them. I was so angry and upset, but I couldn't cry.

There wasn't much that we 'owned' in the projects. We didn't have video games or fancy TV's, but we made do with what we had. We would cut the bottoms out of crates to make basketball goals and would hang them with clothes hangers on the porch. We transformed into mini NBA players. I was good at acrobatics, so when families would get put out, we would take their mattresses into the field in the back and flip. Head over feet, we could rival the US Olympic gymnasts. We played hide and seek, red light-green light, and many other games that were common for kids. These things offered normalcy and made us like every other child in the world.

Due to us not having food, I started hustling. I guess in a sense, this was my start as an entrepreneur. I noticed that people's trash was overflowing outside, so I started asking everyone if I could take out their trash, charging fifty cents for a one-time pickup, and twenty-five cents for multiple pickups. I kept a log and everything... I was my own QuickBooks. I would go to the corner store after I made money and buy me, my sister, and my mom a bag of potato wedges and chicken. I remember feeding my family and having an extreme sense of pride in seeing my family fed and full.

My mom ended up pregnant and gave birth to my brother, who was born premature. My sister and I had to get training in CPR and everything to make sure we knew what to do if he stopped breathing... to take care of him. I was used to checking on my siblings. Most of the time in the middle of the night when I checked on my baby brother and sister, my mother would be gone to the next building to Ms. Elizabeth's to smoke crack. I would go to the end of the building, yelling for my mom in anger and worry, because so much was happening in Dodge City. I'd seen people shot in the head. As my family's protector and provider, I remembered waking up nights, knowing something was wrong, my mom being gone and checking to make sure my sister and brother were okay. One night I woke up, and the front door was open, and there were junkies in our house. My grandmother Hattie taught me to boil sugar and water to throw on people if I ever got scared.

There was so much violence in the projects, and despite her addiction, my mom was still very protective. She loved us as best as she could regardless of what she was going through. I admired her for her strength, even in her weakest moments. People didn't realize the things that you went through along with the internal struggle tied to a habit. I remembered times when people would come through shooting, and my mom would dive on us to protect us.

Going to school wasn't that good either. People at school would tease me because I didn't have new shoes or clothes. Most kids only recognized the differences instead of what caused them. So because we weren't laced in name brand with new shoes on the first day back from break, we became the butt of jokes. They would ask what I got for Christmas, and to save face, I would always say she was getting us something next week... but next week never came. I had two best friends that could relate to what I was going through, John and Reggie. They could relate because of similar backgrounds; little did I know, crack addiction was an epidemic in North Nashville. One would have thought they were the only ones going through the choppy waters until you saw another boat trying to weather the same storm. Bonding over something as detrimental as parental drug dependency wasn't a first choice, but when trying to survive, alliances of any kind were essential. John and Reggie became my crutch because, for the first time, I had someone who understood me.

We weren't what you would label 'the good kids.' Our environment influenced who we became and the behaviors we picked up. We would hunch girls, steal cars, and go across Bordeaux Bridge to Dollar General to steal cologne and clippers. We became experts at dine and dash and often hit Shoney's. With the clippers I stole, I started cutting hair in the projects before school started, to earn extra money outside of the trash business. Believe it or not, I was pretty good and earned a decent amount of money each summer.

In underserved areas, there were always organizations that worked to give the kids something to look forward to. When kids were bored, they would tend to get involved in things that led them down a path of destruction. The idle mind was a dangerous place to be left in. There was a program sponsored by YMCA called Compute and Shoot. It was run by a former NBA player Clyde Lee along with David Suttith, Tim Bryant, and Darryl Caldwell. The program worked with kids from every housing project and inner-city school. We were offered tutoring and go-to basketball practice. The program changed my life. Through the program, we would battle against other teams and were able to channel our energy toward positive things and not focus on the environment that was waiting for us to return. My first real job came through this program with the YMCA on Gallatin Road at age thirteen.

CHAPTER 2

For the Record

> **"I was always a provider even before I could fully understand the word.**

I was always a provider even before I could fully understand the word. I used to work the summer job with the YMCA and saved my money so that I could splurge on me and my sister. I felt like I could handle them talking about me, but I didn't want her to have to deal with it at all. There was one time I worked all summer, saved my money, and went to Bert's downtown. At that time, it was the store to shop at. You always heard the commercials on the radio, "Bert's I'm here." I came home, hid the remaining money in my room, hung up the clothes with pride, and asked my mom if I could go play at my friend's house. When I came back home, the clothes and money were gone. It was then that I realized just how powerful addiction truly was. This hurt because I never really had anything, and I had worked so hard to get these things for myself and my sister.

Not long after that, pain hit me once again. The only person who understood what was really going on was my sister. She told me she was going to live with our aunt. Our aunt, who used to live right next door, had moved about ten minutes away. I was confused and hurt more than anything, because I didn't understand why our aunt didn't take me and my little brother. I turned into another person. I tried to cope with what was going on and cried all the time. My sister and I were really close, and we still were. Our brother was too young to understand what was going on. The truth was, no matter how much pain I had to endure, it shaped the man I became. I guess it was a conundrum... how pain and darkness could be the very thing used to create strength, courage, and resilience. Not knowing it, I would need those very traits for what was headed my way.

I was coming home from John Early. I walked home every day, and this was just like any normal day, or so I thought. When I got to the top of the hill, I saw about ten people ravaging through all these items. As I got closer, I realized that these were our items, and we had been put out. There were strangers going through our things and taking them. What was even more weird was that there was no one there from my family. I was there alone. The only place I could think to go was my grandma Hattie's house. I vividly remembered turning around, and nothing seemed small anymore. I knew then that I had to do more to better my circumstances.

On my trek to my grandma's house, as I wept because of the unknown, I repeatedly said, "I will never be broke again; I will never be broke again." I was in a trance of sorts... focused on changing my life by any means necessary. That moment was one of the most pivotal moments of my life. It was like a transition. It was the moment that was to make or break me. It was the moment that Little Robert became his own man, even if by force. When I finally got to my grandmother's house and told her what happened, she comforted me. I left not long after that and became a child on the streets.

If I couldn't go anywhere else to seek refuge, I could go to my cousin DeDe's house. We all had that family member who was extremely lax and was the 'cool' one. They didn't have many rules, they'd let you drink—maybe even smoke—and they'd bail you out of the trouble you always seemed to get into. Growing up, we always said we would be like them because life just seemed to be too good for them. I started getting high, smoking weed, and hanging with my older cousins. This was when street life really started for me. Of course, we were just doing petty stuff like borrowing money to buy weed and smoking blacks, but that evolved because we quickly started hanging out with the old heads in the neighborhood. We started to use harder drugs which meant more money was needed. It became a cycle. Some of my older cousins lived on 16th and

> **"I was good at school, but I could never focus because of the distractions from my life.**

Buchanan, so we would walk the eight blocks from 24th to 16th to hang out because we thought we were grown. The need for money pushed us to sell drugs, which we didn't know how to do. I made the scheme for me and my cousin, Steph, to meet Montez and Lil' G at 16th so they could teach us how to flip cocaine. I didn't see it then, but I was appreciative now.

They wouldn't teach us at all and would send us back up the street. They might would smoke a blunt with us, but they weren't going to let us stand on the block. Because of their refusal, we started stealing and doing whatever we could to get money to

buy weed. That entrepreneurial spirit had always been in me...
maybe not in the conventional way, but it was definitely there.
I would go to the carwash early in the morning and would help
people wash their cars. I would come back with a bankroll and
buy weed and food for everybody in my crew. I used to also go
to the Shell station to pump gas all day and earn more money.
I had a baby face, good manners, and hustled to get what I
wanted, and it always worked like a charm. Work never bothered
me, and I was always down to earn a dollar.

At this point, school was out of the question. I was good at
school, but I could never focus because of the distractions from
my life. I attempted to go back to school a few times. My family
tried to help me during my time on the streets, but they didn't
realize how far gone I was. The first person to try and help me
was my mother's ex-husband, also known as the catalyst for
us moving to Dodge City. My mom called him, and he tried... I
thank him for that. I moved with him, tried to go to school, and
everything was good for a moment. But eventually, he dropped
me off with my aunt Charlene, who was no longer here. She was
the rock of my family. Even when things were bad, she was one
of the only family members who would allow me to come over.
She would always make sure we would go to church. I owed my

deep roots in faith to her. Aunt Charlene was older and didn't realize I had moved in and begun to sneak out my room on the second floor to go next door to get high. When she couldn't take it anymore, she dropped me off at the Oasis Center. The Oasis Center got fed up, and I had to go stay with my granny. My granny was older and really out of touch with the type of child I was, so I just ran away and went back to the streets. Finally, there was my uncle. He tried to add some normalcy to my life, but that didn't work out. So where did I go? Back to the streets and to DeDe's house... the two places where I had the most freedom. DeDe was my angel. If it weren't for DeDe, I would have had no place to go.

Being back near where I used to hang out put me back in the mix of everything I used to do. Smoking weed. Hustling. Stealing. Getting money. At this point, North Nashville was the mecca for crack cocaine. My older cousins, who used to hate for me to be in the hood, finally broke down, after me begging them, and taught me

> *"Taking my ambition and coupling it with my manners and intellect, I was able to flip and increase my profits quickly.*

how to sell crack. This was when the Thompson Boys used to run the city and had their crack house on 16th and Buchanan. There used to be a line out the door. They were selling twenty-five-dollar grams, which generated a nice profit. Once my cousins taught me, we used to short stop the Thompson Boys. This meant we would catch the sell before they made it to the Thompson Boys' house. They used to pull pistols on us to stop us from "short stopping" them which affected their money. In my hood, they used to have this thing called a 'double up.' Only the wholesale dealers would have this deal. You would go to the wholesale dealer, ask them for a double up—for example, if you have ten dollars, you get a twenty-dollar piece of crack, then you take that twenty dollars and get a forty-dollar piece of crack. When you sold it, you could go to the wholesaler and buy two grams for forty dollars. Once you got a gram, you could break it down and make sixty to sixty-five dollars off of it. This process was called flipping. The reason they would allow you to get two grams for forty dollars was because of the relationship that you had built with them over time. As the wholesaler, I wanted you to come up, because the more you came up, the more you spent with me which meant more money in my pocket over time.

With me being a natural hustler, this process was easy

for me to understand and implement. Taking my ambition and coupling it with my manners and intellect, I was able to flip and increase my profits quickly. But even with all that hustling, my age hindered me. Not really understanding the true power of money and being fueled by my habit, all I wanted to do was get high.

This was an okay time in my life. People may read this and think how could being a fifteen-year-old selling drugs be "okay." But you had to realize, this was the first true stability and consistency I had had in years. Looking back now, I realized that I was still in a dark storm. I had some stability because I was staying with my cousin, school was still of no interest to me, and I missed my family, but I was free to do what I wanted to do. I would often see my mother because she would come down the street while I was on the block, but the relationship wasn't as strong as it once was. She was still my mom, I was still her baby, the love was still strong, but the streets had changed us both.

CHAPTER 3

Survival of the Fittest

Being in the streets in North Nashville and the more I hung out on the block, I quickly learned the meaning of only the strong survive.

Being in the streets in North Nashville and the more I hung out on the block, I quickly learned the meaning of only the strong survive. So here I was, fifteen years old, out on the block, 24/7/365 trying to flip this thing we called crack. Competition was everywhere. On every block, you had crack houses. All of North Nashville was infested with drugs. Either you were doing them, or you were selling them; and in some cases, it was both. So not only did you have competition, you had to look out for robbers who roamed all hours of the day and the police who were constantly patrolling because of the increase in crime. Because I was so young, the robbers and police thought I was an easy target. I stood out because of my age, so I had to stay on the move constantly. I couldn't stay in one place too long or else I would get caught. I would have to run at least two times a day from the police, but as soon as they gave up the chase, I would go right back to the block to make more money. The block had worn paths where people had walked back and forth between the alleys and the main street through people's yards. Worn or not, they proved to be the quickest way to dodge the police.

No matter what happened, how much you had to run, or the craziness you witnessed, you would always return to the block; whether you were there to buy or there to sell, there to rob or there to tell. The thrill was the cheese. We were the mice, and the hood was the 'trap,' literally.

In the hood, everybody was a nephew, everybody's baby needed shoes, and there were more sob stories than *Young and the Restless.* You couldn't imagine the stories I'd heard... the intricate webs that people spun to pull on your heart's strings, so you'd lower your price or give them something for free. People would tell you that they didn't have any money, but I was so focused on the bottom line that I took change and all. All money spent, regardless of its form. Those who were hustling on the block had a common goal: get money. There were so many of us that when customers would pull up, we would run up to the car. It was like a track meet, and the prize was making the sell. Everybody would pull out their rocks to show who had the biggest rocks and even slap rocks out of each other's hands so the customer could focus on ours. But everybody that had a big pack didn't automatically have good product. There were some people selling 'overs'—putting twenty-eight grams of cocaine and an ounce of baking soda in a Pyrex jar in a pot of boiling water to cook it. You would put about two teaspoons of water inside the Pyrex jar to slowly cook the cocaine, turning it into crack. This method was called dry cooking. Utilizing this method of cooking, you were able to double what you initially put in and increased your profits. The only downside was that your product would be weak because of the extra soda you put in to stretch the cocaine. People would know your dope wasn't good because of the residue that was at the top of the crack pipe. Even though you would make the initial sell, the customer wouldn't buy from you again. Keeping it as pure as possible, even though it cost more, made for repeat customers which meant more consistent profits—beating the competition.

We couldn't have drugs in the places that police would automatically search. You had to hide your product so that, in the event of a search, you'd still be able to walk away with what you had. People got creative with their hiding places, including me. We would sag to hide the crack between our butt cheeks. It wasn't a secret. It was a neighborhood trend.

Even in doing all of this, I noticed that I wasn't getting ahead. Like I said earlier, junkies were creative storytellers. They built a rapport with you and then hit you with a story that made you question what your name was. Because they had become consistent customers, they would come to get dope on credit. Nine times out of ten, you would never see them again. So much for a solid relationship. If I had to guess how much I left out on credit, it would be like losing fifty thousand dollars or more. That was a lot of money to leave on the table because Lil' John John 'nem baby needed formula or diapers.

> **Losing out on money because of credit would affect your re-up.**

Losing out on money because of credit would affect your re-up. When I couldn't re-up, I would break into houses. But not just any house; I would break into the dealer's trap house. I would be up all night anyway. I would wait until they would go home to their families and clean house. I would take scales and everything. My block was cutthroat. In order to survive, I became a part of the culture at the time. Could you imagine a city within a city or never leaving a street for two years? Everything I needed was found within walking distance of 16th and Buchanan. It wasn't until I was almost twenty-two years old that I learned how to go outside of North Nashville, even to Antioch or to Rivergate Mall. You could get a person to do anything for some crack. I didn't have girlfriends, no car, nothing. I quickly learned that this little crack rock I had gave me power. I was having sex with grown women before I was even grown. If I needed to go shopping, more than likely at Sam's, I would use crack to lure a driver. People would pawn their cars to me. They would beep me, and I would call from a pay phone and take them their car back.

My cousin, who I was staying with, caught wind of what I was doing in the streets. I had to leave her house because she didn't want to be around it. I started staying on the streets, sleeping in crack houses and even cars. As with everything, you couldn't be doing all this wrong without a host of arrests. At one point, it felt like I was going to juvenile every other week. The first time I went to juvenile, it was over something we started out of boredom. We created a game called "Let's Go Beat Up a Junkie." What was fun then, now rendered me speechless. It should have never been a thought, let alone a game. It was embarrassing to say that we were doing this. We were hurting innocent people who had done nothing to us. We were wilding out. We would take a brick and break people's windows out. Eventually, we got caught, and I got arrested. I was scared because I never thought I would be encountering this. Strange enough, my mother came and got me the first night I was there. She was extremely mad and cursed me backward and forward. She was so hurt that I was there. Sadly enough, it wasn't that scary because this began my life of crime. When I could find my momma to come, she would come. There was one time she didn't come. When your parents didn't come pick you up, they would put you in state's custody. I went to Woodland Hills for a period of time then to a group home. Five hours after getting to the group home, I was back on the streets. Not because I was released for good behavior or because my sentence was magically reduced, but because I ran. Regardless of when I got arrested, if there was a window of opportunity to run, I took it. I even conned a state deputy to drop me off in the hood instead of taking me to

> **Just like in everything you do in life, especially when it comes to running a company or wanting to break into an industry, you need a mentor.**

the group home. I have run from every group home they put me in. Name one, I ran from it.

Just like in everything you do in life, especially when it comes to running a company or wanting to break into an industry, you need a mentor. I felt like if I wanted to take it to another level, I needed to get under somebody's wings to get to another level. So, I met Chico. Chico was a big guy and a boss. I was smart, so he took a liking to me. He liked the way I moved, and he took me under his wing. Initially, we just drank and smoked weed, which eventually led to me lacing my weed—putting cocaine on our weed for a bigger high. Back then, we called it "chevy's." He could cook dope like no other—on the stove, in the microwave, in a coffee cup—it didn't matter. Despite the tough love, he taught me a lot. He gave me a new perspective of what it meant to survive out here in these streets alone. I started to see how shiesty things could get. One night, I was out late, minding my own business, when some guys pulled up, robbed me, took my dope and money, and hit me over the head. I immediately told Chico whose abrupt question was did I see their faces. I didn't. They were masked up. He told me that I needed to get something to protect myself. Even after being on the block all that time, I didn't have a gun, but the risks were getting bigger, and nothing was worth me losing my life. After that robbery, I got a gun.

CHAPTER 4

Pullin' the Trigga

My lifestyle continued to spiral. Not only did I have to watch out for police that constantly circled the block, but I also had to deal with people who were watching me, looking for a quick come up. These people were lazy and didn't want to hustle. They only wanted to watch a hustler like me make a living and then wait for an opportunity to try and take it from me. Back then, my mentality was you had to kill me to take my stuff, which was an ignorant thought. But, I was young and wild. Who in their right mind wanted to lose their life over a couple stacks or something materialistic? Thankfully, I was not the man I used to be.

The first gun I purchased was a .22 automatic. I bought it off the street for seventy-five dollars. You couldn't tell me shit. I thought I was the baddest mothafucka alive. Back then, everyone wanted to make a name for themselves, and I wanted everyone to know who I was. Call it ego or just a cultural thing, but I wanted to be known.

When you thought about it, almost everyone nowadays was seeking some type of noteriety, so things hadn't really changed. I would carry my gun and sometimes shoot recklessly in the

When you thought about it, almost everyone nowadays was seeking some type of notoriety...

air and at random things. As crazy as this was, this was my reality. I went everywhere with my gun and was earning respect from my hustler's mentality and charisma. At the age of fifteen, I lost my cousin, Montez. He was killed in a pawned car, riding with neighborhood friends.

The way it happened was, one day Montez and his friends pulled up to a junkie's house to collect on a debt. They made the junkie get in the car and then went to the ATM to get their money. On the way back to his house, my cousin began arguing with the junkie while they were in the back seat. They began to wrestle over a gun. The driver pulled over and as they were exiting the car, the junkie shot Montez in the back of the head.

The junkie said it was because he was scared.

Montez never wanted me on the block, but due to my persistence, he ended up teaching me things about the game I had never forgotten. When he died, it was a big blow. Losing someone that close to me made me heartless. It made me feel like I had to stay on my toes and defend myself at all times. When he passed, my aunt Charlene tried to help give me some normalcy and let me move in with her. So I moved to Antioch, TN and went to Apollo Middle. Moving to Antioch, I got the nickname Trigga because I always had a gun on me. People who met me didn't understand my reality. I had been on my own since thirteen, so I had been self-sufficient. My mentality was I had to protect myself because there were people trying to manipulate me everywhere I went. I had become heartless.

I met this old head by the name of Glock. Glock was an OG who took me under his wing. Being around him gave me validity on who I was as an individual. Sometimes we hung at a studio. What hood guy didn't want to be a rapper, right? One day, we were at a studio up the street, and I met up with Ny'Quil, who was a friend of the studio's owner. I needed to make a run, so I gave Ny'Quil money to get me a quarter ounce of weed. When I came back, I walked in to see him sitting at the table rolling up weed. I approached the table and asked for my sack. He handed me a sack that didn't have a quarter ounce of weed. We then got to arguing because I knew he was trying to slick rob me. I pulled out my gun and threatened to shoot him. He was a grown man, and I was fifteen. I remember having a stern look in my eye as I pointed my gun at him. In the end he got scared and ran out the house, and I earned my nickname "Trigga." As crazy as it sounded, I was proud to have the name. I wore it like a badge of honor.

After being in Antioch for about eight months, I ended up meeting a girl by the name of Tasha. Tasha was sexy. She was the first real girlfriend I had, and she was now my oldest daughter's mother. I didn't know if she was attracted to me or my reputation, but we had a cool relationship. Being in Antioch, gave me a sense of hope and stability. But I was too far gone. My mentality, heart, and focus had changed… I felt like I was a grown ass man and demanded to be treated as such. My aunt tried her best to give me a home, but she didn't really know how much pain I had endured by being on the streets so long. I was missing my mom, my sister, and my brother. I felt alone. Not having them around hurt, but I masked it. Looking back, I started to act out. But my aunt didn't play any games. Everyone knew she would whoop ass. She whooped me more than I could count. She had really bad asthma, so she didn't whoop me and my cousin as much as she did when we were younger. Despite that, she still ran her house with an iron fist. Me being me, I started sneaking out of the window to get out of the house. I would unlock the first story window, go to Glock's house, and get high. I would then sneak back in the first floor. She caught on pretty quick. When she would catch me, she would put me on punishment, which made me rebel even more. What took the cake though was a year prior to that, I sold a gun to a friend who shot himself in the foot. When questioned, he told the police he got the gun from me. I was at school skipping class when a white man approached me and called me by my name and told me we had a lot to talk about in which I questioned what we had to talk about. We went into the office, and he told me about the gun and the shooting. He handed me a card and told me to give it to my aunt. Trying to avoid trouble, I didn't give her the card. But she eventually found out anyway and sent me to the Oasis Center. I started to reflect back at the Oasis Center and wanted to change. I called and asked if I could come back, and she said I could.

But even after that I ended up sneaking out of Oasis Center

with a friend and walking up to Edge Hill to get some weed and got high. As we were walking back we ended up getting caught and got put out of the center. I called my aunt crying because I really wanted to go back. Tasha was there, and I really missed her. Luckily, my aunt let me come back for a little while… until my next fuck up.

We went on a church retreat held at Duke University with people there from all over the nation. We stayed in the dorms on campus, and I was in the room with one of my friends. As bad as it sounded, we wanted to get high at the church retreat. We never went to any of the programs, and when people would leave, I would go through the dorms checking for unlocked doors. I would walk in and steal anything of value. We would walk to the store across the street, and I would tell them, "hold on, I'll find us some weed." I would then walk up to a stranger to ask for weed. I could easily spot the weed man and get served. We got high in our room and bought candles to try and mask the odor. My aunt's son was there as well, and he even started to smoke with us.

One day while we were smoking, my aunt walked over and found us. She spotted my cousin with a blunt in his mouth in the cafeteria. Ultimately, they knew who orchestrated it, and when we got back to Nashville, I got put out. My aunt looked for somewhere for me to go, but to do us both a favor, I ran away before she found a place. I caught the bus back to 16th & Buchanan. It was just me and my gun again. Back in the hood with no money, I chose to start robbing and stealing with Trigga as my official name.

CHAPTER 5

Function & Flow

Junkies. It's funny, growing up, that's what we referred to our customers as, with little regard for the people that they actually were. These were the people who worked, took their earnings and then bought from me and my friends. And since we had a product that they craved, they continuously put money in our pockets. They say repetition is the mother of skill, but they rarely address the mastering of what skill was being repeated. If you repeatedly draw, you'll become a master artist; continually speak to large crowds, you will become a master speaker; continually hustle, you'll become the king of the streets. Where we put our

> **They say repetition was the mother of skill, but they rarely address the mastering of what skill was being repeated.**

energy, repeatedly, is, logically, what we'd master and who we become.

The saying "You are who you hang around" was so very true. Back then, I surrounded myself with people who liked to get high, so smoking weed was normal. I was young and impressionable, so I followed suit and joined in on the action. Being on the block day after day became a necessary routine that lost its thrill quickly. My day was hustle, make money, sell out, and re-up. It was a cycle that became habit. We all watch the movies that show the glamorized version of street life. The hustler makes all of this money, buys all of these expensive items, and balls out. You rarely see the grittiness of it… the truth. You rarely see that being a hustler is as strong of an addiction as doing the drugs and often leads to more undesirable, detrimental behavior. I started getting high to keep myself entertained. I smoked cigarettes, weed, laced weed… anything I could to get high. I was chasing paper and an emotion that had escaped me. It got to the point where being

> **"You rarely see that being a hustler is as strong of an addiction as doing the drugs**

sober didn't feel right to me. Getting high and making money were the only things me and my friends cared about. We even started smoking weed with cigarettes because we thought that it gave you an "enhanced high," not knowing that smoking can potentially stunt your growth. Maybe that's why I'm so short now. ☺

One night after playing basketball at the park, I went to the nearby pavilion to get high. This was where people, some young, some old, went to get high. Even though still considered a baby, our crowd would smoke weed that we bought from the alley. With little regard for getting caught, we would walk up to the fence, hand someone our money, and they would hand us a manila folder full of skunk. At first, the skunk was all we needed to get high. But as with everything and every child, we were in a rush to be older and have more than we did. We eventually went to hang out with the older folk in the pavilion and started to get high with them, and it was at this point that I was introduced to powder cocaine.

I snorted my first line of cocaine when I was fourteen.

I snorted my first line of cocaine when I was fourteen. Looking back on it, I really didn't know why I enjoyed the high from it. It seemed to just make me paranoid, but I think I was only into it because it was the trend. I thought I was gaining respect because I was finally hanging with the big dogs, doing what they were doing, when I was really just being stupid. I got addicted to cocaine not too long after I started using. When you become an addict, your time was consumed with trying to figure out ways to get more of the thing you're addicted to. Because of this, the time that I normally used for relaxing and chilling became preoccupied with me trying to figure out how to get more money to buy more drugs. I had become a junkie. But you couldn't tell me and my friends that; we were all doing it. We would actually treat the junkies like they were beneath us, but we were all the same. We would have "get high" parties where one person would bring the weed, someone else would bring the cocaine, and someone would bring drinks, and we would just sit around and get high. We went from getting high in the little park to getting high on the block. The more we spent on the drugs, the more we needed to sell to get more money. It became a vicious cycle. Get high… sell dope… make money… get high again.

At sixteen, I started staying up all night in the dope house selling and getting high with my friend Chico. As my addiction to drugs continued to grow, I also developed a sex problem. Sex and drugs were constantly on my mind, so that's what I spent most of my money on. As long as I had enough money for drugs and sex, I was in heaven. My addictions continued to grow which caused my appetite for drugs to expand. When smoking cocaine on my weed wasn't enough, I started mixing the powder with nicotine. When I didn't have powder to put with the nicotine or money for weed, I would crush up cocaine and put it on the cigarettes.

> **I kept this part of my addiction under wraps because if my childhood friends knew I was doing this, they would have talked badly about me.**

I kept this part of my addiction under wraps because if my childhood friends knew I was doing this, they would have talked badly about me. I'd done pills, marijuana, cocaine, crack cocaine, and even heroine. Being honest and transparent about the situations I'd been through involving my life and past addictions were the first step toward my recovery.

I also witnessed my mother struggle with addiction. There

were times when I would be standing on the block and I would see my mom sitting there waiting for me to give her some money. She would say she was hungry, so I would give her some money and actually see her walk up the street to buy drugs. At one point, I went to a crack house to catch some sales and walked in to see three to four people lying on the floor. I was shocked when I found that one of the people on the floor was my mother. Despite our actions, her love for me never faltered. I never sold her drugs, but some of my family members did. They sold their own mothers drugs. Even though we were both involved in the drug game in one capacity or another, my mom never smoked drugs in front of me, and I never sold in front of her. If a sale was in front of me at the same time as my mom, they would have to wait to get served. I was very judgmental of my mother then, but little did I know we were both in the same boat. It amazed me that I could see my own mother battle with addiction and not recognize that I had chosen the same path. But you live, and you learn.

Losing many of my friends to a drug overdose and witnessing my mother's addiction had brought me to the point in my life where I had no choice but to be a voice of reason for young people dealing with addiction. It took me a long time to get to a point where I could talk about these things. Call it ego, denial, or pride; whatever word you choose, I would agree. I didn't recognize that my past actions qualified me as an "addict" until I was about thirty. As I reflected on what I had been through in

My name is Robert Sherrill, and I was an addict.

my life, I knew that I needed to change. I thank God that I made it through this dark period in my life so that I could now share my experiences with you. It took me a long time to admit that I had a problem, but I can now finally admit it. My name is Robert Sherrill and I **was** an addict. I hope that my story would motivate you to take action and never give up if you're struggling with addiction.

Addiction was a taboo topic. It was something that most people shy away from and rarely want to discuss. We felt that being an addict made one weak without understanding that facing and conquering a mountain as big as addiction, actually made one strong. I'm not perfect, and my past wasn't pretty, but my truths made me the man that I was today. There are a lot of things that I experienced that would break many, but I feel it gave me the foundation I needed to reach the goals that I have.

Being an addict was something that I was ashamed of for a long time. The perception of addiction was never positive, especially when dealing with drug addiction. You never know the journey of the person next to you... you never know how dark their past has been or how bright their future would be. People look at me and don't see the child of my past or the man of my future; they are focused on my now. But my now was a direct result of my then. There was a newfound sympathy for addicts. 'Junkies' has become an offensive term, and the focus has shifted from problem to solution. The idea of condemning one race over the other based on the same behavior and actions has become a 'bad thing' to do. We've come so far as a nation, in this right. If you know someone who is struggling from addiction, call the Drug Abuse Hotline at 1-877-879-2013.

CHAPTER 6

My Brother's Keeper

Growing up in the projects, I met a lot of cool people. Some were associates, some became family. A lot of people were just forgotten when we moved away. With so many bad memories, I figured why hold on to negativity and bad relationships. One person, I wanted to hold on to however was my play sister, Stephanie. Stephanie lived down the walkway from us in Dodge City and was actually a distant cousin. We grew really close early on and spent a lot of our years going through the same struggles of being raised in the projects, coming from broken homes and drug addicted family members.

During my mom's addiction, we would go up the street to one of her friend's house who she would get high with, and while we were there, we would meet her friend's brother named Terry. Every time we went there, Terry would have on a white shirt, some Dickies, and would be rolling weed. He would always pick the seeds out of the weed, and I would watch him. As inquisitive as I was, I asked to hit it one day and coughed my lungs out. But nevertheless, me wanting to be down, I hit the blunt again.

My mom was in one room getting high, and I was in the other doing the same thing… shamefully. Terry and I developed a real cool relationship, but life separated us. We would later find out that our respect and relationship would remain the same even as time passed. Funny how the story goes. Fast forward four years to me living with Tasha, my first daughter's mother, in Tennessee Village. I was trying to do the family thing, which I did for a while. I had just gotten back from the country; more on that in Chapter seven. Tasha was my ride or die. She came to Knoxville to get me when I got hot. She drove three hours there and brought all my stuff—a loaded AK47 and a pit-bull named Chaos—back to Nashville. I had nowhere to go, so I moved in with her in UC in South Nashville. I was going to visit my sister in Jo Johnston and saw a car roll up the street with someone that looked like Terry. So I yelled, "Terryyyyy…." And he turned his head and came back. We hugged like we hadn't seen each other in twenty years, although it wasn't quite twenty. We caught up and asked all the questions… how you been…? etc. He gave me his number, and he called me the next day and came and got me. I wasn't expecting what was to come.

While I was staying with Tasha and hustling, a guy came and knocked on the door. Lesson: trust no one and be your own best friend. He called me and said he was coming to get some weed. I knew him, so I didn't suspect anything wrong, and I wasn't worried about anything happening. It's funny that the games we play, end up playing games on us. I let him in. He looked at the weed, and he had a gun on him. I grabbed the gun, unloaded it, looked at it, put the clip back in, popped one in the chamber, put the safety on, and gave it back to him. *That's how he should have been carrying a gun,* I thought. However, since he was my little homie, I wasn't tripping. I allowed him to go outside and bring his homeboy in to get the weed. As this was going on, I was in my boxers, Tasha was upstairs, and her two kids were in the room sleep. He drew down on me and said, "Where it at, where it at?" My mind immediately went to thinking about Tasha and the kids. They took me into the kitchen, tied me up, and kept asking me "Where is it at?" I was in shock because my little

> *It's funny that the games we play, end up playing games on us.*

homie set me up. Two more people came in, so now there were a total of four robbers. They started going through the house. At this point, I was still in shock, so I wasn't giving them the right information. Tasha was pregnant with my daughter.

They ended up bringing her downstairs. The whole time, there was a big guy standing over me swinging a tech 9 telling me he was going to kill me. One of the other guys brought a sheet downstairs and threw it over my body like they were going to kill me. They were rummaging through the house threatening me constantly. All I could think about was Tasha and the kids. They kept bringing up me having something to do with his cousin getting killed. They used it as a reason for the robbery, but I was confused. He keeps saying 'I'm gon' kill you.' My real nigga shit kicks in. I was young, stupid, and didn't give a damn. I grabbed the sheet behind my back and poked my head out to look him in his face. In my mind, I was thinking if you're going to kill me, I want to see it... whatever that means. I needed to watch him do it. Every time I poked my head out, he kept pulling the sheet back over my head. They finally found what they were looking for, came back downstairs, kicked me, and left out the back. Tasha was in the living room, I was in the kitchen, and the kids were upstairs. I untied myself and checked on Tasha and the kids. I immediately called Terry. He showed up thirty minutes later, and we went to retaliate. From that point on, we were inseparable.

We moved from UC. For the moment, Tasha moved back with her mother, and I moved with Terry and Stephanie, who were now married with kids. Crazy, right? We both were OCD, loved smoking weed, and were natural born hustlers. A match made in heaven. Our slogan was "it's time to take over the world," whether it was robbing or selling drugs. We tried to embody that slogan. Walken has to be acknowledged because he was my brother as well. He was white, but he was still our brother. He was talented, could rap, had manners, and was good with the kids. But Walken was someone you never wanted to cross. The three of us became something like the Dream Team. If we wanted it, we either bought it or took it. Simple as that. We didn't care about the consequences.

If we wanted it, we either bought it or took it.

One day, my crazy ass wanted to take something. Granted, I was hustling, but taking was easy. I had this dude and girl who claimed they wanted dro. I called them and set up a deal to sell two pounds, but we were really about the rob them. But my, how the story gets deep. This was an example for everybody who wanted to rob, of how things could go bad really quick. As I was planning to sell two pounds, I didn't know that they were CI's planning to bust me. We didn't find this out until later. This is a book, so here goes the story. We hollered at one of our customers to rent his car. *Crazy thing is, I'm still cool with him.* He didn't know what we were going to do, so I didn't blame him for what he did. We got his car, set up the deal, plotted out our escape, and we executed it perfectly. We pulled up, I got to the car, and they asked for the weed.

Me being the finesser at the time, I said, "My homeboy has the weed, and he stays in this apartment, but since he doesn't know y'all, y'all have to give me the money and let me take it to him to get the weed." They went back and forth about giving me the money. I told them, "Y'all know me, it's cool," and they finally ended up giving me the money. The moment I hit the breezeway, I took off running and heard tires screeching. I ran down the stairs, over a hill, and jumped over a creek to where Terry was in the getaway car in another apartment complex. I hopped in the back seat and ducked down. Miraculously, we got away... not knowing that I just robbed the police. The celebration started. We got the money. We added it to the stash and kept it moving. A couple of days later, we got a call from the customer who pawned us the car. He was wanting to meet us to get some crack. As we went to meet him, we pulled into a restaurant. It was a dead end, strategically picked.

Once we pulled in, we couldn't get out. All of a sudden, we were surrounded by TBI agents in unmarked cars and trucks. They hopped out, snatched me out the car, and beat the shit out of me. As it was happening, I was yelling "I'm a juvenile," but they didn't care. Their response was, "Did you know you robbed the fucking police?" They whooped me out of my shirt and shoes, and I went to juvenile and my brother went to jail. But me being me, I had my money stuffed in a sulfur 8 grease can. The police went to the house and searched, looking for drugs and guns. When I called home, Stephanie said they were trying to get my brother out of jail. I told them about the grease can where I stashed my money, and they used that to get my brother out. They sent my butt to TAFT, which I couldn't get out of. I did two years at TAFT Youth Development Center, and upon my release, I went back to stay with my brother. Not long after my release, my brother and Walken were accused of a double homicide, which detectives came to see me about on numerous occasions. I ended up having to testify on his behalf. I'm sad to say, my brothers were both serving a double life sentence. I was out here on my own after that. I had to find my way. I missed my brothers, and I wanted them to know that I loved them, but I kept them green dots flowing and plenty of money on my phone for them to call. He just called while I was writing this chapter and was thrilled about being "Terry." ☺

CHAPTER 7

Making of a Hustla

I was taught the game early. One thing I knew about the game, there were no rules. It's play or get played. Shoot or get shot. Grind or starve. It was up to you to pick your poison, but in the end, it was all poison. I was a born hustler. As far back as I could remember, hard work never intimidated me. That characteristic alone was unheard of nowadays. At an early age, I developed a hustler's mentality.

> **"One thing I knew about the game, there were no rules. It's play or get played. Shoot or get shot. Grind or starve.**

I cultivated it and added other characteristics to it. This created an enormous cocktail of hustle that resided in me. I learned that people had different hustles. When you looked at selling crack, stealing, or robbing someone, each person doing the deed had one goal in mind: the come up. You wanted to leave each of these scenarios better than when you entered. Even though, at this point, I didn't agree with those scenarios, I understood them all the same. I guess that's why I didn't understand broke

> **"Drive, ambition, dedication, and consistency were all required to effectively hustle.**

individuals. There were so many ways to hustle. People need to understand, it's not the hustle, it's the individual. Each hustle was based on the individual. Drive, ambition, dedication and consistency were all required to effectively hustle. Regardless of what your hustle was, with these four things, you would make it. Again, why was half of America broke?

I didn't understand why I chose to play the "game" for so long even though the winner was already chosen. It was a game that I was never meant to win. What was it about humans that makes us play a game that we know we are going to lose? What was it that was so unattractive about playing a game where we made the rules and worked toward a desirable outcome? I'd yet to figure that out. Circumstances create the type of hustle that you choose, most won't agree, but it's a proven fact. And that's my reason for being a hustler.

Growing up, seeing my mom on crack, never having money, never celebrating the holidays, never having designer clothes and shoes did something to me as a child. If you recall in chapter one when we were evicted, I made the vow that I would never be broke. At my age, I couldn't go get a job, so I chose the next best thing, or so I thought, getting it how I lived. Whether stealing, robbing, or selling drugs money was the motivation. From the time I learned that I could double my money from buying a twenty-five-dollar gram, when prices were good, and make sixty dollars or sixty-five dollars, I was hooked. Where else could you double your investment in as little as an hour? I didn't have to pay taxes or overhead... the money was all mine. Even with the perks, I see now, everything that glittered wasn't

> **"For me not to have made it far in school, I really should have been a mathematician."**

gold. When we hustled, we often lost sight of reality. We didn't see who our hustles hurt, and who it affected. The fast, easy money and the lifestyle sidetracked us.

Especially when money was something that you worried about for so long.

For me not to have made it far in school, I really should have been a mathematician. I was digitally weighing cocaine, buying wholesale, and selling retail. I even could have had a brick and mortar store. Finally, I found something in the drug game that fit my character. It was safe to say my circumstances cultivated a real hustler. I was running up and down 16th. Despite me getting high and gambling, I would always bounce back. I could wake up broke in the morning and have two or three hundred dollars by nightfall. I could go from a twenty-five-dollar gram to buying a quarter ounce in a day selling pieces.

There was so much dope in the North Nashville community, every side street off Buchanan, from 17th to 16th to 14th to 12th to Cephas to 10th were flooded with cocaine. It was nothing to wake up at 3 a.m. and find dope in North Nashville. You had heavy weights on every street, and when I say heavy weights I mean bricks. My life was consumed with the game. I guess it was unavoidable. Despite being robbed, shot at, and losing my money, I became addicted to getting it all back. It almost became less about the money and more about the system of the hustle. When I said system, I meant the buying, manufacturing, reselling, and profiting. I started to take the game seriously when I met some OG's. By OG's, I meant the guys who took me under their wing like Chico, Glock, and Terry, my brother. But for this next phase, it was going to take some heavy hitters.

One of my first OG's in this period of my life, as I was getting older, was Four Eyes. I met Four Eyes in my younger days. He had the weed and stayed on 23rd Avenue N, where my grandmother lived. Everyone else was scared to buy some from him, but I was seasoned. I knew when to talk, when to shut up, and when to make a move. I approached him to buy a fourth-ounce of weed one day, but I didn't have all of the money, so I asked to take the weed and bring the rest back later. Based on my reputation in the streets, he let me skate. I went back to my friends, took some of the weed out and when they gave me the money, I took him back the money that night. Your word was everything. That got his attention and respect. After that, he would come through the block and would yell for me every day.

Another one of my OG's was Kazz. Kazz was like family. I call him an OG because he stayed in my ear about positive and worldly stuff. Things I needed to hear. He balanced me out. I learned then that your circle must be small and diverse. He had me thinking on new levels and looking at life a unique way. He was a hot emcee when I was growing up. He was a member of the group Ghetto Soldiers. Being close to him, I learned to rap. I was pretty good and recorded my first album. I was working at Looby as a lifeguard at a summer program at the time. He brought me the tape so that I could hear it and I was floored. I rode around for a year straight making people listen to it.

Two of my other OG's were named Boddie and Jason. I met them on 16th and Buchanan. They were really cool and were always together. Them being local artists and me learning to rap spurred our connection. Things started to get deep when I met these two. Everyone loved me because I was different. I was advanced for my age. At this time in my life, things started to pick up. I went from selling crack and weed to selling heroine. And it turned out Boddie and Jason were slanging as well. We got a house and started getting money together. When crack was slow due to a drought, which happened once a year, it made cocaine scarce in the city. When demand was high and supply was low, prices skyrocketed. This was what the drought was. Strangely enough, the drought would always hit around Christmas. No one wanted to get caught by the drought, so people diversified their hustle. If you had cocaine during the drought, it was going to be a great Christmas for you. The money you would make would increase drastically because everybody prayed for a plug during the drought.

This particular drought, we had heroin and it was doing numbers. So much so that I had to move to West Nashville with Boddie and Jason. I learned some of my dope house etiquette from Chico. With Boddie and Jason, things were serious. During the drought, most jack boys would kick in your door and take what you had. I was taught to run a tight ship at this point. We had walkie talkies, cameras, and doors that you couldn't kick in. You answered the door with loaded guns and pointed the gun at the door before you opened it... that's how serious it was. Boddie and Jason were no joke, and they made sure I knew the ropes. This went on for a while. Sometimes I would get arrested and get sent to a group home. But I would always run away to find Boddie and Jason again. The funny thing is, during this time I never thought about school, prom, or playing sports. My childhood was non-existent. I never went on a family trip, never knew my times tables. Hell, I barely knew how to write. But I knew coke prices, quality control, manufacturing, marketing, selling, and running crack houses with no problem. Wasn't that something? Jason and Boddie would leave me in the crack house every night and would go to their real houses with their girls. I had nowhere to go, so the trap house was my home. I would clean up, get snacks, and hold it down with three pit bulls as my body guards. I would sleep with a shotgun and handgun every night. One night there was a knock on the door... I did my normal routine and made a sale. What I didn't know was that this customer had gotten some money from another person who ended up being with Vice. Two days later, we were in the house in bullet proof vests making beats on the beat machine when we heard a loud boom. Suddenly shotguns were in our faces. It was the police. The house it turns out was being raided. We all went to jail. Since I was a juvenile, I got sent to a group home which I ended up running away from. Jason made bond, and Boddie had to do time because he violated probation.

All of my OG's were very influential in my growth as a hustler but none more than Loco. I met Loco through Four Eyes. He was definitely a different type of dude. We related to each other a lot because we were so much alike. Slick, stylish, charismatic, and full of ambition. Loco was heavy in the streets. Like Boddie and Jason, Loco was an artist as well. For some reason all of my OG's were connected to music. I met Loco when I was fifteen, but we had often had previous encounters. When I turned eighteen, we started to kick it a lot. I really looked up to Loco and tried to impress him because he was international. We would go to this small town, hours away in the country and everybody knew him. They ate out of his hand. He was like a local celebrity. The country shit was different, and I liked it. Being with Loco gave me instant fame. I was a city boy with golds and braids. The girls, culture, and city were all more attractive than what I had experienced before. The thing that really shocked me was that the prices were extremely high. The same twenty-five-dollar gram in Nashville would be one hundred dollars in the country. If I knew then what I know now, I'd probably be locked up in the feds for the rest of my life along with Loco. The money was so enticing I probably would have never stopped. I made my home down there. Looking back on it now I see now that Loco was intelligent and charismatic enough to run this country town. When you embrace your ambition and focus in on your actions you can really make things happen. In the beginning I walked around town with ten to eleven ounces of crack that Loco would cook and bring back overs. The dope was mediocre. He would make four and a half and bring back seven ounces that I would have to work. I would run through seven ounces in two days... all pieces. When Loco saw that, he wouldn't let me out of his sight. I was almost trapped in a sense. But I respected Loco so much I didn't complain. I did it without him asking because I knew he wanted me to.

I just continued to sell dope because I was making real money. So much money, I bought four cars, a spot in Rockwood, and a spot Harriman. So I was set on not coming back. Loco introduced me to a girl name KeKe. KeKe and I got real close, but there was nothing sexual about our relationship. I learned a long time ago, you get further making a woman your sister or your friend. Sex always complicates things. KeKe was a hustler. She shocked me because she had a hustler's spirit and was very charismatic, which goes hand in hand with the game. Sometimes the coke (product) wasn't as good as you say it is, but you must have enough charisma to sell it anyway. KeKe had the "know how" so I made her my right hand. As an evolving 'boss,' I quickly figured out the system. Loco loved me because I was a rider, and I didn't ask questions. I made money and always answered the call of duty. I figured if he was happy, I needed to make myself happy too. So I would accept his high priced, mediocre cookies of crack. When I say high, we would come to Nashville and go through my plug to get drugs for Loco paying five thousand dollars for a nine piece which equates to 550 dollars per ounce. Taking all the risk, I would follow him back to the country with the drugs on me and get charged one thousand dollars an ounce. Not only would he double the price, but he was cooking it in such a way that got him more overs. Loco was making money hand over foot off of me. KeKe and I decided we would leave and come to Nashville and buy our own nine piece. I would cook it and sell it along with Loco's product. I didn't see a problem because he was still making money.

After a couple of months, Loco started to act funny. I didn't know who told him or who reported to him, but like I said, he was a celebrity in the city. He was cunning and manipulative and knew how to corner people. I was slick myself, and he knew that, so he would definitely keep tabs on me. He knew I was capable of taking over because he had seen me do it before. I was making so much money in this city that I had to call Terry and Walken to come get cash to take it to Nashville. I was always taught to keep a stash. I started to feel that Loco was getting jealous of me. Partly because I was getting all his ex-lovers. When he pulled up somewhere, they weren't speaking to Loco, they spoke to Trigga. He couldn't stand it, and one day he asked me to take over.

That day Loco asked me and KeKe to come to Nashville to get a nine piece. We ended up staying two days so that I could see Tasha, my baby girl, and my family. I had plenty of money, and I was the man. Instead of rushing back, I sent KeKe back to the apartment we had together with the phones and the cocaine. The next morning, I woke up to a phone call from KeKe telling me that someone broke in our house and stole our cocaine. In my head I was like these "country niggas don't know who they are messing with!" Walken, Terry and I hit the interstate to go to the country with an arsenal. We pull up straight to the apartment, and I put KeKe on the spot because I wanted to know how this happened. We rode around, pistol whipped a couple people, shot at some people but couldn't get any answers. I packed up some things and took it back to Nashville. When I got back to Nashville, I told Terry that I had to go back and get the money. I went back by myself and a friend told me that Loco was getting jealous and sent some people in my apartment and that I needed to quit messing with him because he couldn't be trusted. I didn't want to believe it because he had taught me so much and was like a big brother, or so I thought. During our last conversation his posture and tone didn't feel right to me. The night before I left, he asked me to meet him at the store, and when I met him the police pulled up and arrested me as soon as he pulled off. I'm thinking he tried to snitch. I sat in jail a couple of hours and made bond. I then called Tasha and told her to come get me. She said she couldn't get there until 9am the next day. So when she pulled up she put my belongings along with my AK47 in her car. I didn't put it up until I got out of the town because I didn't trust Loco anymore after that. Once I got back, I got heavy in the game. Those grams and fourth-ounces that I spoke of earlier were crumbs compared to where I ended up.

Back in the city, I picked up where I left off. The game was changing, and I had become more conscious of it after the Loco situation. Mistakes are there for you to learn and grow. I am more protective of my circle now. I started to take music more seriously. While going to court for something minor, I saw two men in the elevator. As we were riding it I was sizing them up, and they were sizing me up. They saw my tattoo on my forearm and asked me what I "knew about that." So I start to explain, and it sparked a conversation. We both figured out we both did music and decided we would go to the studio after court. The older brother was Brandon and the younger brother was Marcus. Little did I know that this would start a long-lasting brotherhood that I still hold dear to me. It was not without its ups and downs though. I could tell by Brandon's lyrics that we played in the same arena. So I approached him after we finished the song to see if he could be a potential customer. From then on, we decided to team up and take over the scene together. They were a little younger than me, and I had a car, so their mother would bring them to me and drop them off. I would tell her I would watch out for them and not to worry about anything. I became the big homie because I looked out for them because they were younger. Brandon was just as sharp as I was… Marcus not so much. But it didn't matter because Brandon and I looked out for him. We were like two peas in the pod. We were from two different sides of town… me from the north, him from the east. I was a GD, and he was Crip. We were in two different gangs that hated each other, but green was our gang and that was understood from the jump. Some of my friends wanted to rob him and some of his friends me. But we would never let that happen, we had too much respect for each other. We told each side that one better not touch the other. If you want to hurt a man, hit him in his pockets, and they knew that if something happened they wouldn't get any more dope. We went from meeting at the courthouse, to recording music, to them spending the night over my house. Tasha would fix us full breakfasts at 2 and 3 am. We became close like brothers, and we still are to this day. The older we got, the more ambitious we became. Making of a hustler became an understatement. We became authentic brick boys. What I didn't know was that after a brief hiatus, Brandon was the man. He didn't want to tell me, but after a couple days, he came clean. Brandon had stumbled up on a serious plug. I didn't know how real it was until he picked me up and we took a ride. We touched every part of town and by the time we got back to the house there was money all over the car. I had never seen that much money in my life. I wanted in. At this point, I had money, but not like that. We decided to team up and go hard. And go hard we did. Between our networks, we flooded the streets. It was a time when I felt like sixty percent of the dope in the city was coming from us. Not the quantity, but in who we were selling to.

> **"One thing about me, I always wanted to see people win.**

One thing about me, I always wanted to see people win. This was a downfall of mine, but nevertheless, I liked to see people win. So I brought my cousin, Lil' John, into the game. Lil' John was a hustler too. Not only did I have a right-hand man, but now I had a left one too. We became a family. Brandon brought in the work and we distributed the work. Just like Loco, Lil' John was a master chemist. He could cook cocaine like no other. There would be so much cocaine that we didn't have to put overs on it, but Lil' John was so good at it that we could drop in nine ounces, get back twelve ounces, and it be gone in forty-eight hours. That was three extra ounces which was pure profit. The money was coming so fast, we were cooking half birds for the fun of it to see how many overs we could get back. Off each flip, before we sold anything, we would have a free four or five ounces off half a bird. I never would re-rock cocaine, but I would 'shol' put some overs on it. At this time, we were selling ounces for five hundred dollars, and my block was on lock. We had crack houses throughout the city because we wanted to stay lowkey. But with that much money it was hard. Everybody would run their mouth regardless of the threats made. So eventually, everybody knew we had bricks. The gangsta in me embraced it. So we loaded up on more guns, brought more cars, and more phones in order to avoid confrontation which leads to beef. We didn't want beef because it wasn't good for business. But unfortunately, beef, wanted or unwanted, was an inevitable part of the game.

"The game was stressful and having protection was my peace.

I was at my spot one night alone with my mac11. When I was selling bricks, I kept an AR in my hand and 9mm in my pocket since I would normally be in the crack houses by myself. The game was stressful and having protection was my peace. The glitz and the glamour overshadowed the stress and risk. It was about 2 am and I was laying on the couch with the mac11 as usual. Something told me to get up and get in the bed. I knew this was God. I grabbed my gun, went to my bed, laid on top of it with my gun beside me. I normally lay under the covers, but this night, for some reason, I just laid on top of it. Crazy thing about it, it's almost like the army, you go through possible scenarios. In all my crack houses, I was always prepared for worst case scenarios. In this game, uncertainty was certain. Around 3:30 a.m., someone kicked my door in. I didn't know if it was my spirit or my intuition, but I knew it was going to happen. As I play it back, I was prepared for war. The moment the door busted open, without flinching, I grabbed my gun and let off about ten shots down the hall so that whoever it was knew I wasn't playing. I just wanted to hit whoever was in my house. After I stopped shooting, I turned on the light looking for a body. I walked outside looking for someone and didn't see anyone. I knew two things were about to happen at this point, either reinforcements were about to come, or the police were on the way. It just so happened that I was messing with a chick who stayed in the same complex. I called and asked her to come help me do something. Once she arrived, I loaded half a key, some big scales, five guns and twenty thousand dollars in cash in a backpack. I tried to get her to take it to her house because I knew the police were on the way. God must've been watching over me because as soon as I got the backpack on her and explained what to do, the police walked in and asked what happened. I said someone kicked in my door and started shooting. They asked for our id's and I asked 'why do you need my id? I'm the victim?' They said they had to check to see if we had any warrants. I knew I had money and could get out. When the two police officers walked to the squad car I stayed on the 3rd level and told her to go to her apartment, and she left. Five minutes later, the police came back and asked where she was. She had given them the wrong social, and I had a warrant, so I ended up going to jail. All of this because someone wanted what I had and decided to kick in my door.

I started moving no less than ten bricks a week. Most people didn't understand that that wasn't a lot of money when you're in a wholesale type of business. Being a wholesaler, the profit margin was slim. The off shoot was minimization of risk and headache. When I started to really progress in the game, I had to give all my crack sells and four and a half and nine piece sells to smaller dealers. So I stopped selling crack all together and would just deal in kilos. At that time, I was getting bricks for eighteen thousand. We weren't the only game in town, so I couldn't make my margins too big. I didn't want to hold any product. I wanted to get it, drop it, and make my money. I was selling bricks for nineteen thousand and five hundred or twenty thousand depending on the buyer. Some dealers would hold on to the dope just to get more money. But I felt like if I could sell ten bricks for nineteen thousand and make one thousand profit off each one in a couple of days, that was a winning formula. Opposed to me selling bricks for twenty-one thousand, while a three-thousand-dollar profit, it would take forever to sell it, and I'd have to figure out where to stash it and that maximized the risk of getting caught. And like all good things, they must end. The thing about the game was you got pulled in, and before you knew it, you got swept away by the current. Some were able to get out in time... others get pulled under. Sink or swim...

CHAPTER 8

Busted!

I always wrestled with the term 'the trap' because I couldn't figure out why would individuals continuously do something with a predetermined result. Was the money that good? Was the lifestyle that good? My answer was hell no… but it always wasn't that way. I'd watched people lose their life from being murdered and in prison. I watched families get destroyed and kids growing up without a father who was pursuing money. I didn't know if it was the money or the status that I was addicted to. It was something about walking around and everyone knowing who you are that's enticing. That is until you get caught.

> **It is something about walking around and everyone knowing who you are that's enticing. That is, until you get caught.**

As a hustler, you dreamed of finding a plug. The plug was

like oxygen. It was essential in order to grow and expand your operation. But strangely enough, your plug was not always loyal. Most of the time, your plug got jammed and would leave you holding the stick. There was no loyalty or love in this game we called 'the trap.'

Brandon and I were heavy in it. We had crack houses all throughout the city. We were well known, and business was good. We had just received some marketing materials for our first CD that was set to release called "The Investigation." Looking back, it was as if we spoke our own demise into existence. I was

"Looking back, it was as if we spoke our own demise into existence.

headed to the trap house, and Brandon was in the parking lot excited because our posters had just arrived. He popped the truck and said 'Bro, its official. We out here.' We celebrated for a minute, and I asked what he was about to do. He said he was going to make a run and that when he got back we would go put the posters up. I almost went with him, but he had a car full. I guess it wasn't my time. He was on his way back after taking care of business and got pulled over. He got caught with a half a brick and ten thousand. I went and made his bond which was about nine thousand cash. We lost that money and not only that, he eventually got locked up for the charge. All of our dreams and aspirations about music went down the drain because we functioned as a group.

A week after he got locked up, I got a call from the plug, Martinez. He was asking me to meet because Brandon owed him some money. I was nervous at first because I didn't know his intentions, but he asked me to come by myself. So I strapped up and met him on his turf. At that point, he told me that some things were lost and that I had to make it right. I had to do it because I needed him. What I told him was that if he gave it to me, I would work off Brandon's debt and then start back doing business. He agreed. So I hit the streets and made it happen. The thing about Martinez was his product wasn't always the best. I would have to cut corners to make do. Sometimes I would have to call him back to have him bring me new work because the work I had wasn't jumping back. This meant that what I sold to customers wasn't producing what it should after they "cooked" it. For example; if they dropped twenty-eight grams in the pot and it cooked down to twenty-four grams, it was a four-gram shortage.

They would call me back, mad that they lost money, so many times I would have to make it right. This went on for some time, but despite the pitfalls, I started to excel. I was at my peak moving thirty birds a month. But like I said, I was only making 1,000 to 1,500 dollars off each one. But the reward definitely outweighed the risk.

When you're getting money on that level, everybody is trying to come at you to get drugs. Some of the customers are good… some are bad. But sometimes you have to go through a trial and error period and take a loss in order to figure out who is who. The dope was coming in so fast. I wanted to see the people I grew up with get money too. I would front them four and a halves, nine pieces, etc. And I would have to hunt them down for my money. I never understood this. If I'm helping you and I'm looking out for your best interest, why not pay your tab on time. Sometimes, I took total losses when they would get busted, and I would have to make up for the difference. I would have to go in my pocket to get reup money to get right with Martinez which caused us to get into it a couple of times. I had to start confronting people who owed me in order to make sure my plug was straight. I remember I was going to the Jeezy concert and ended up running into Jacob, a guy from the hood.

Jacob was well known in my hood and he was a little older than me... but we knew each other. Now that I think about it, I was talking to another guy from the hood, and as soon as Jacob walked up the guy walked off. I should have known something was up. Jacob started talking about how I looked like money and how he brought Jeezy here etc. He asked if I had some work, and we ended up exchanging numbers. A week or two later, he called and wanted four and a half ounces. We met at a McDonald's, and I let him get four and a half for two thousand and five hundred dollars. Everything went smoothly on the first trip. A week or two later, he called me for nine ounces, I met him at his job gave him the stuff and left. But on the way back to the house I noticed I was being followed.

I went the long way home and ended up at the trap house in East Nashville. When I walked in, I told my homeboy 'I just fucked up.' He asked what I meant, and I told him I thought Jacob was the police because I noticed some people following me once I left him. I told him I drove around for an hour before coming there. He tried to keep me calm telling me 'If they were the police they would've busted you by now.' I sat there and put my hands over my head and repeated 'I done fucked up.' I was thinking about the money and concluded that if he really was the police, I would have been arrested. A couple of weeks later, he called for a half brick. I made him come to the studio to meet this time. I wanted to watch his moves more closely and make sure he wasn't the police. It was another successful buy. On the last buy, he called and asked for a whole brick. By then I had switched plugs. Martinez had gotten busted about five or six months prior to that. I hit up my new plug and told him that I needed a brick. He was about to go out of town and told me he would meet up with me. When I pulled up to meet Jacob, I had my new plug in the car. Jacob knew my new plug and told me that he didn't have the money. He said he had to run up the street to get it and asked us to come with him to get it. Now that I think about it, he was trying to lure me into a school zone. While he was gone, he met with detectives and told them that he knew my new plug. He said, 'he got the man with him.' They told him to come back with the money. He came back, got in the car, I gave him the brick and he gave me a wad of money. I asked him 'what the hell is this?' If you know anything about making transactions of this size, the money is usually neat and rubber banded in stacks of ten thousand. The wad of money didn't look like five thousand when the transaction was for twenty thousand. Something was off. Of course, you know what happens next. Detectives swooped in. Cuffs on wrists. They put

The mugshot from my arrest on federal drug charges.

The Journey Back to Now   **93**

Jacob in the back of an unmarked car with no handcuffs, and me and the new plug ended up in the same car together. Once we got downtown, there was no sign of Jacob.

I sat at CJC for two months trying to get a bond reduction. My bond was five hundred thousand dollars. Finally, my lawyer got me a bond reduction to one hundred thousand dollars... I paid ten thousand cash to get out. I ended up giving my lawyer ten thousand. A month later, the feds picked me up. My attorney couldn't represent me federally, so that ten thousand was a complete waste. I didn't have representation at the time. I ended up getting an appointed attorney through the federal system who told me 'I was screwed.' I remember asking the feds when they came to pick me up how bad was it and they said, "Mr. Sherrill, it's bad." I didn't know how serious it was until I saw my paperwork and it read: The United States of America vs. Robert Sherrill. When we went to court, they had to call the ambulance for my mom. Honestly, I was so hurt knowing that I wasn't going to see my kids. And after seeing my family cry and seeing my mom get taken away in an ambulance, all I could do was cry.

For the first time in my life, I felt helpless. I saw the people I loved the most, hurt to their core, and it was all my fault. There are no words to describe how that feels. I was sentenced to sixty months at eighty-five percent if I didn't get in trouble.

Inarguably, the darkest and worst day of my life became the best day of my life.

CHAPTER 9

On the Yard

The federal system is different from the state system. I was used to going downtown, getting booked, fingerprinted, and making bond. We had a phrase, "I'll be out before the ink dry!" but this wasn't the case this time. When the feds came in, they took me to a new location. I knew I had messed up. We drove past the CJC, made a couple of turns and ended up at a building I'd never seen before. I was in the front seat of Titan pickup truck. Riding with this big body building looking white man with dark glasses and an FBI vest. They weren't as bad as they looked... or maybe that's just my opinion. When

> **I took a lot of deep breaths and thought about life.**

we parked, they unstrapped me, asked me to step out, and they took me through a tunnel, up some stairs to an elevator that took us to some floor. They put their guns in a safe, and we went through this door. I was handed off to another FBI agent who asked me my name. After confirming my identity, he simply told me 'You've fucked up...' "How bad?" I asked. He told me three and a half kilos. All I could do was drop my head because I knew I was in for it. I wanted to call my family, but they weren't allowing us to make phone calls. After I was fingerprinted, they put me in a holding cell with some other men who had gotten arrested the same day. As we shared a couple of stories, hoping that time would pass, we began to wonder if we were going to stay there the night. An agent passed, and we asked where we were to go from there... he simply said "Stressville." I was like "Stressville... what the hell is that?" He told us it was a lottery pick and that we had to go. Nothing could be done about it.

There are three federal holding facilities. One in Springfield, TN and two in Kentucky. And it was just my luck that I ended up at the worst of the three, but I was mad at the world so bring it on.

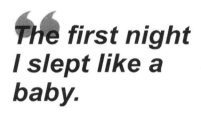 *The first night I slept like a baby.*

During the ride, which was really only forty-five minutes, I took a lot of deep breaths and thought about life. I thought about how we only have one life and how we can be so careless sometimes taking risks that can mess it up. I thought about my kids and my family. The funny thing is that it typically takes a horrible situation to force us to reflect on just how precious life is. I was upset and disappointed. Disappointed that I got caught, disappointed that I didn't listen to my intuition about Jacob... disappointed in my decisions. I always thought I was smart enough to beat the game. I changed phones, switched cars frequently, kept a low profile and kept my circle small. I had all the cheat codes and they helped... for a while. I figured that I would keep winning, but I was sadly mistaken. As we approached Stressville, all my emotions started to take root. I felt mostly hatred and shock. I thought long and hard about the world beyond the walls. We entered processing and were told that the kitchen was closed. Regardless of my efforts they kept saying 'the kitchen is closed.' All I could think about while in handcuffs was eating. It was just a bad situation. We went through processing and was denied my phone call. I was receiving short answers from everyone, and I was exhausted. The first night I slept like a baby. I couldn't believe that less than twelve hours ago I was a free man, and now I was in an orange jumpsuit with flip-flops laying on a cot surrounded by strangers.

The next morning, I woke up to 'chow time' and hopped up because it had been nearly twenty-four hours since I'd eaten. When they handed us our plates I just knew that I wasn't staring at a piece of bread, a half of a banana and some jelly…it couldn't be. My eyes must have been playing tricks on me. Reality had set in. The shock was gone, and I could finally observe my surroundings. As I looked around I could see that there are a lot of skinny people there with no commissary bags.

I asked someone if it was like this every morning and they said 'yes…every day, same meal.' It confused me that there weren't any inmates complaining about the food. They acted like they were just content. Like this was the Stressville "standard of living." I wanted my phone call.

I got a court appointed attorney, Kathleen Simpson. When I was able to call my wife, I tried to call Kathleen on three way, but she didn't answer which infuriated me. And unfortunately, I took it out on my wife before asking her to move some things around. Since my phone call was about to end, I asked her to keep calling Ms. Simpson, and I would call her back. I consider myself to be a pretty tough guy, too much doesn't surprise me after what I've been through. After a couple of hours of hearing other inmates claim they are "the man," lunch time came and I'm even more distraught at my plate. I had a bag of chips and a cold bologna sandwich which I ate. I needed the calories otherwise I would have been well on my way to becoming a skeleton. I was finally able to get Kathleen on the phone, and I told her that I couldn't spend my time being held in this place. She told me she would see what she could do and four days later I was sent to Bowling Green, Kentucky. God must have smiled on me. I thought I was in Heaven compared to Stressville. It was more of a communal system... an open bay instead of individual rooms. I made a call and got some money. There was a commissary, and the food was decent. It wasn't gourmet, but at least it wasn't Stressville. I even found some people that were from Nashville and connected with them.

I ended up having words with a tough guy who acted like he ran shit. At the time I didn't think it was serious. People would always try to lighten the mood or laugh it off to avoid something happening. And it never really turned into anything, but that day I was just fed up. Some people were coming back from the gym and I was laying in the bed. And this particular guy came in and changed the channel on the TV. If you've ever been to prison you know most fights on the inside start because of either the phone or the TV. This would be the first of many. I hopped up and put on my shoes. But before I could get my footing, he hit me and broke my jaw. We got to jacking and fought for about five minutes until the guards maced us. Then they threw us in the hole. I didn't know my jaw was broken until dinner was served and I noticed I couldn't eat. I knew something was off when I leaned to the left and my jaw moved. I asked for the nurse who gave me Ibuprofen, but it eventually wore off. So for five days, I sat in the hole with a broken jaw and no pain relief. They took me to the doctor to get me an x-ray and discovered that my jaw was broken. Instead of taking me to the hospital and taking care of it immediately, they took me back to the jail for two more days with more Ibuprofen. For SEVEN days, I had a broken jaw. Eventually they handcuffed and put me in the back of squad car to transport me to Nashville. I had never been so happy to see a doctor in my life.

This was my first surgery, and I was nervous. I had never gone under the knife, and I kind of wanted my mom. They were treating me so bad. If something happened to me there was no one there to make sure they were doing what they needed to do. I mean I sat in a cell for seven days with a broken jaw! They rolled me back into surgery and gave me something through an IV that made me feel like Jesus had just returned. Thank God, the surgery went well. I remember waking up being nauseous with my mouth wired shut. I couldn't talk, and I could barely breathe. I was also on oxygen. Thirty minutes later, they put me back in shackles and drove me back to Kentucky. All I could do was pray. I had to man up. But things were about to get even worse.

When I got back to Kentucky, I could barely walk. I was wheeled into a room and was so out of it I didn't even notice that I wasn't in the same place, I was back in Stressville. Bowling Green said they couldn't administer the medicine I needed after surgery, so I was sent to Stressville instead. I was placed in a one-man cell, and because of the condition of my jaw,they placed me on a twenty-four-hour lock down. I woke up the next day, sober and furious. For breakfast they tried to give me hotdog water. Imagine trying to raise hell with your jaw wired shut. My anxiety instantly kicked in. During surgery, they realized I had to eat so they pulled one of my teeth out to insert a small tube so that I could take medicine and eat. Everything I was eating was pureed. Pureed carrots, pureed peas, and mashed potatoes all in water form. I had no choice. The narcotics they were giving me were making me sick, but they didn't care. I had to endure the stomach pain and the diarrhea that came as a result of the narcotics. Admittedly, this was one of the worst moments in my life. After a month in solitary confinement, the train going to the federal penitentiary finally came. I rode for seven hours from Stressville to Forrest City, Arkansas, where I served the remainder of my time in federal custody. Processing took about ten hours. After that I thought I would go to my cell, get comfortable, and use the phone, but I was placed back in confinement when I returned because they viewed me as a risk and liability due to my jaw being wired shut.

Because the system is so screwed up, the prison didn't receive any info on my medical condition or diet restrictions. So for the first day and a half, I had nothing to eat or any pain meds. I was also put in a cell with a Hispanic guy who couldn't speak English, so I couldn't hold a conversation. I ate carrots and creamed potatoes while he enjoyed hamburgers, chicken, and tacos for the next month and a half. Some days I would watch him run in place for hours which drove me nuts. Finally, I got fed up and asked the guard if I could see some nail clippers to cut my nails. I had to sign a form to get them, so it took a while. When they brought them, I washed

In federal prison, it is about what region or city you're from.

them in an effort to sterilize them. Then I single-handedly, unwired my mouth. Two days later, I begged to see the nurse to let her know that I could be released since my jaw wasn't wired any more. They threatened to write me up for damage to federal property because I had unwired my mouth. But I didn't care... getting out the room was more important. They sided with me and finally, I was able to hit the yard. The compound was really big. When you are coming out of segregation or processing, you have a white jumpsuit on. Everyone can spot you. As I'm walking to my assigned dorm, I can see everyone watching me. This is what happens when you're inside. Everyone wants to know who you are and your story. When I put my things down, five people walked up on me and wanted to know who I was, what I did, and how long I was there. It checked out for some, but for some it didn't check out at all. Not everyone was free to move about the yard due to being in rival gangs or a snitch. I immediately went to the phone but found that it didn't work since I wasn't programmed in the system. I had no money on my books, so I couldn't use the phone. All I could do was wait. I didn't know anyone to ask for a three-way call, so I had to play things by ear. After three days, I was finally able to connect with my family and tell them everything I needed. My new life as an inmate had officially started.

The first day on the yard I got connected with a lot of people from Tennessee. In federal prison, it is about what region or city you're from. People who were from your area became your homeboys. If you were from Tennessee, you were all in the same car together. But geographically we were all separated.

The real money on the yard was books of stamps.

Then there were the gangs. This was only on the black side. On the white side, you had the Peckerwoods, the Arian Circle, the Arian Brotherhood, and Arian Nation. On the Hispanic side, you had the Aztecas, the Mexican Mafia, and the Texas Syndicate, Northanyos (northerners in Spanish). Each organization had assigned seats in the cafeteria. You've never seen segregation until you've seen this type of living. Prison had its own way of doing things. Its own code of ethics and its own economy. The respect level was real high. People didn't skip you in line, everyone waited their turn because they knew things could spiral out of control at any moment.

The Mexicans ran the yard at the prison. Both the Mexican and white inmates hated black inmates. But if you asked everybody else, they would tell you that the blacks ran it, but that is a lie. I became friends with one of the Mexican Mafia guys and asked what the beef was between Mexicans and blacks. His response was "Look around. Y'all are too loud." And as I observed, we were loud like he said. In prison, your own homie would cross you before the Mexicans or the whites. They kept to themselves. We didn't mess with them, and they didn't mess with us for the most part. But in prison something was bound to go down. There were transgender men and even closeted gay men who would go to visitation to see their wife and kids knowing they were in a relationship with someone on the yard.

> **The most lucrative thing to do in prison was gambling.**

The real money on the yard was books of stamps. A book of stamps had twenty stamps, and you could get a hold of as many stamps as you wanted if you had the money. Each book of stamps was worth six dollars. Whatever you wanted to buy, whatever you wanted made, a leather belt, a picture of your kids, shoes or even a radio, stamps were the way to get it. People that worked in the cafeteria would steal bell peppers and onions, chicken patties, and open a mini market in the dorms. People would buy what they wanted in order to make what they wanted for the night. It was reminiscent of a side street market. Some inmates had stores in their cells. If you didn't have money, there were 2-for-1 sales were inmates would keep a record of what you owed them. There were some guys in there who were culinary geniuses who could make pizzas out of tortilla shells. Some guys would cut trash cans in half and make stingers. They would get oil from the kitchen and make deep fried burritos. Some of the main meals people made were burritos, tuna nachos, and fried rice. I can't lie… it was good. My cellmates and I would barely eat from the kitchen.

The most lucrative thing to do in prison was gamble. There were bookies who would pass out tickets while people placed bets. This is what kept the peace most of the time. Tattoos were also big business. Some of the best tattoo artist were Mexicans. But only certain Mexican gangs would tattoo blacks. Most of my tattoos came from the Mexican Mafia and the Texas Syndicate. In order to get a tattoo from them you would have to sneak in their dorm and hope that you didn't get caught. If you were caught you got written up. Each morning when I would go for a jog I would see Mexican gang members sharpening knives and hiding them just in case a war popped off. I've been through many gang wars in prison. And gang wars are just like those movies like Braveheart where people run into each other and clash. I've seen people get stabbed and beat to death all over something petty.

Speaking to someone on Monday and seeing them carried out on a stretcher on Tuesday does something to you mentally. Prison is a scary place. No one wants to live under the constant threat of losing their life or worse, taking a life defending their own. Talk about post-traumatic stress syndrome! Oh, and I can't forget to mention the free labor generated by being in prison from a thing called Unicore. They work you all day for only eighteen dollars per month. Everyone signs up for it because that is the only way to get money and essentials that you need in prison. Things like detergent, deodorant, etc. I have two words to describe Unicore, legal slavery. To add insult to injury, you also had to deal with rejects that were from the Army and police academy. These individuals added another unnecessary level of stress to the situation due to having their own issues. A lot of them seem to take out their frustrations on inmates. Note to America: Everyone wasn't meant to be in positions of authority.

Last, but not least, there were so many different religious practices in prison, I couldn't keep up with them all. I learned so much about the different "pop-up" belief systems that people had while I was inside. It seemed like I was always combating some new religion that wanted to put itself up against Christianity and my beliefs. I became the go to guy on theology. I learned from my mentor Michael Flemons who's a genius. He taught every class on the yard.

If you are reading this and this disturbs you in any way, then being a criminal wasn't for you. Prison made me realize that freedom is a luxury, its precious. It's something that you can never take for granted or get back if you act carelessly and have it taken away from you. I thank God for prison and for the tears I shed. I thank Him for the nights I couldn't sleep and the years that I lost I can never recoup. They say that regardless of the storm, the sun is always shining. But despite the obstacles I faced, the inmate I was in prison made me the CEO I am today.

CHAPTER 10

The Transition

The transition from prison to CEO wasn't easy. The first thing I had to do was become adjusted to being out after my release. Most people follow the rules and catch a bus as you're supposed to when you are released from prison. But here I was, fresh out of prison, and still breaking the rules. When I was released my wife and father-in-law were in the parking lot waiting for me. It didn't matter to me that this was against the rules because I missed my family. I couldn't see myself on the bus, finally a free man, and surrounded by inmates. I had served my time and was free. It was time to act as such. I took one deep breath

Some people slip into pitfalls and pay with their lives, others pay with their freedom.

when I stepped outside and looked around and told myself I'd never be back. Being locked up is not a life that a normal person would want to live. Despite the hardships one goes through or the laws you may break, no human would willingly want to spend their time being told what he/she can and cannot do. I thought when I was released that the first thing I would want to do would be to get something to eat, but I wasn't that hungry. I was nervous because I knew that now I had to piece back together the life I left behind. We are so selfish and think that it is all about us, but we never think about those that do the time with us. With all that on my mind I knew I had to rebuild in order to take care of my family. I was constantly wrestling with my thoughts. I was excited for a new beginning but anxious about what was to come. I really didn't know where to begin. I had nothing. No clothes. No money. No car and no license. If you can visualize that, then you can kind of get an idea of how I felt as a man.

Being afraid is a topic that men stray from. Everyone claims to be fearless, but being afraid is what keeps you alive. A certain amount of fear can help you avoid the pitfalls that have devastating consequences. Some people slip into pitfalls and pay with their lives, others pay with their freedom. In both cases, there is loss. Being afraid and also being aware of the inevitable, unavoidable, and potential outcomes of certain situations forces you to make more rational decisions. You could say that with wisdom came a bit of fear. Sometimes it takes years of life experiences to get to the point where you recognize that the price of doing something is not worth it. You pick your battles, and you start to move differently.

These are some of the things that ran through my head on the way back to Nashville. I didn't speak much on the way back because I was focused on the repairing and rehabilitation of Robert. Home wasn't home, I had to go to a federal halfway house.

I made one stop to see my Aunt Charlene before I went to the halfway house. This stop was unique in its own right. If you recall in Chapter four, I mentioned that this was the aunt who, despite my troubled youth, prayed for me and told me that everything would work out. The morning I turned myself into the feds I stopped by her house and she anointed me with oil before I went into custody. It was remarkable to end up back in her house on my first day of freedom... full circle. I was excited to see her... she would write me, send me a card or drawings during my darkest times. Even though she was not an artist, her drawings of stick figures with glasses made me smile. I love my aunt and truly miss her. Even though I'm able to share my story and capture what she meant to me and my family, it hurt not to have her here.

I knocked on her door, and we embraced in relief. It even started to snow which made the situation more angelic. The snow didn't stick, but the flakes were coming down pretty hard. She sat me down, and we reminisced about the crazy things I did in my youth. We talked about everything... my mother's addiction, the trouble I got into when I lived with her, my choices. She told me, "Robert, I always pray for you, and Aunt Charlene never would give up on you." I told her I learned my lesson. I didn't know that that would be the last conversation I would have with her. She left shortly thereafter to go to her heavenly home. I was on one of my weekend passes at my mother-in-law's when I got the call that she was gone. I remember getting to her home and seeing her body on the floor... it was a surreal moment for me. I couldn't move. Despite the limitations, I am happy and thankful to God that I was released when she passed so that I was able to say my goodbyes.

Finally, after our talk, I arrived at the halfway house tired and hungry. I had made up in my mind before that I wasn't going to eat any more of the food. I didn't get to see my kids before I checked in, but after getting settled my wife brought them to visit. That was the happiest day of my life. I didn't realize that me being gone had affected my children in a major way. It took time for my youngest baby to deal with me because she didn't really know who I was. My other girls were excited to see me and happy that I was home, but there were underlying issues and things with our relationship that I wouldn't realize until later on. The city had changed a lot since I left. I was eager to get back into the swing of things, but the system and the way it was set up made that impossible. Everything had red tape and hoops that you had to jump through in order to do simple things.

The halfway house was no different than prison. The only difference was there being a TV and a phone you could use to talk. Ordering food was a major upgrade from my previous accommodations. But for seventy-two hours I really couldn't do anything. A lot of the guys at the home still had a "penitentiary swagger" which blew my mind. I didn't have a lot of money, but I wanted the good deodorant, a new wave cap and new boxers. Simple things that would make me feel normal again. So I started asking where people worked because I knew I needed a job. I wasn't allowed to go back to work for my company. Talk about a hindrance! Since I was in their company, I had to follow their rules. Eighty-five percent of the guys in the house didn't have jobs, so most of my questions went unanswered. I knew what I needed to do and how to do it, but I had to wait a couple more days until I met with my counselor to put my plan into action. The moment I got classified and was removed from the seventy-two-hour restrictions, I was able to leave from my new prison. My wife was at work, so I had to catch the bus. I hadn't caught the bus in years. In my early years I would never be caught on the bus, but my ego was now gone. Tough times show the content of your character and who you really are.

> *Money was limited, so I had to make it stretch.*

The first place I went to was Demo's, and when I got there I was given an on-the-spot interview. The next stop was Maggiano's Little Italy. Two days later, both jobs called, and I didn't have anything else to do so I took them both. I worked 6:30am-3:00pm at Demo's and 3:30pm-10:30pm at Maggiano's. Everyone was in an uproar because they didn't understand how I had two jobs after being out only three days. It was simple to me. I went to my interviews dressed appropriately, with sense, a dress shirt, a tie, and some slacks. The crazy thing about it is that the managers couldn't believe that I was dressed like that just to get a job at their restaurant. Sometimes you really have to dress the part to impress. The managers at Demo's had personalities that I had to deal with. The head manager made me go buy makeup to cover-up the tattoos on my hands and neck before I started working. This caused all of my shirts to have makeup stains on them at the end of each workday. I hand washed my shirts by hand every night.

Money was limited, so I had to make it stretch. When you want something bad enough you put up with things that you normally wouldn't. Why make mountains out of molehills when your eyes are on something far bigger? Maggiano's hired me as a host, which was fine with me. I had plans. I didn't start off washing dishes or bussing tables. My first job there was as a food runner. I eventually became a table busser. I had four job codes at Maggiano's which meant I could do four different jobs in the front and back of the house. I found out I was able to make more money at Maggiano's because I was able to pick up double shifts. So since the money was good, I decided to quit Demo's.

This meant more money and more time away from the halfway house… a win win if you ask me. I worked the hardest I've ever worked at Maggiano's. That job pushed me to the limit each day. There was always something I learned every day. But given enough time, I developed a method to the madness. After working there six months it was time for my evaluation, and they ended up giving me a twenty-cent raise. This broke my spirit. The reason this bothered me so much was because I could see the possibilities of what your salary could be if you were in upper management. And this showed me more than ever that my background and prior mistakes would always be a speed bump in life. We say that you should not hold someone's past against them, yet society shows that at every turn your past is all but forgotten. I would have to call the halfway house to report making it to work and when I was leaving to return home. In between shifts, the halfway house would call to make sure I was at work. What business would want to deal with that?

> **❝ I learned to be consistent in my ambition, stay focused despite distractions, and become dedicated to a cause greater than myself.**

Despite the ups and downs at Maggiano's, I was a rock

star. I received the employee of the month award twice, and I liked my other coworkers. I'm actually still friends with some of the people I worked with there. During the time I worked there I realized God had other plans for me. I believe that having to catch the bus and deal with people who looked down on me because of my past was God breaking me down and pruning me for greatness. People who knew the old Rob who had money now witnessed me bussing tables and pouring their water. I'm sure many were in disbelief that the infamous "Trigga" was cleaning tables, but it all worked out for the good. I learned to be consistent in my ambition, stay focused despite distractions, and become dedicated to a cause greater than myself. I learned that the opinion of others does not maktter. Expecting people to be there for you only sets you up for failure, so you must learn to rely on yourself. This is why character is very important and must be developed.

After a year, I left Maggiano's for good. I had set my eyes on greater heights.

CHAPTER 11

Developing a Mystery

The best part about a mystery is figuring out how to solve it. In the beginning, we didn't have all the pieces we need, but somehow the puzzle always ends up complete. The thing is, you can only solve a mystery if you are willing to work at it, sometimes tirelessly, until you get the solution you are looking for. It wasn't easy—it could be draining—but I could promise you that it was worth it.

Prior to me serving time, I owned a janitorial company named R&R Cleaning with Ronnie. One R for me and the other for Ronnie. My brother-in-law was someone I trusted. When I was in a gang, it was hard for me to trust people, but I tested him on more than one occasion, and he always passed. I decided to bring him in as a partner and purchased a cleaning franchise with my money. I purchased the franchise from a company named Anago. The owner was charismatic, like one of those infomercial guys fresh off of TV. He had a big smile and a lot of enthusiasm. But behind the smile was a lot more. I was excited to be an entrepreneur. I thought I was making my way.

He taught us how to strip and wax floors, how to clean carpet, and how to provide superior cleaning solutions for various types of businesses and buildings. I already have OCD, so it seemed fitting that I would purchase a janitorial franchise.

Starting over wasn't as easy as I thought.

I continually excelled at my duties and grew R&R Cleaning to grossing twenty thousand dollars per month. At this time, I didn't have any employees. It was just Ronnie and myself. Ronnie was a great person, but he was lazy. I decided to split the buildings between us as the company continued to grow. That way we controlled our own destiny. I am a get it done kind of guy. Instead of working the third shift, up at odd times of the night, I would have rather start a second shift and be done by third shift. This split was actually the beginning of the end of our partnership and the company. Because of Ronnie's oversights, he began to get complaints at his buildings which cost us contracts. I saw all of this coming, but having a big heart hurts you in the end if you were dealing with people who didn't have the best intentions for you. Focus and drive differ from person to person, and I learned its best to make tough decisions early on. That way you can avoid the consequences of choosing the easiest more comfortable route. Because I chose to overlook the obvious, Ronnie lost eighty percent of the company including contracts that we had secured when I went to prison. When I was released from custody and was able to start back working for R&R, there was no solid foundation to build on. I ended my partnership with Ronnie and R&R, and I started a magnificent company, Imperial Cleaning Systems, Inc.

> **A wise man once said, 'do what you can with what you have where you are'...**

Starting over wasn't as easy as I thought. It made me realize that there was a lot that I didn't know about building, developing, and operating a company. If you would have asked me prior to me serving time, I would have confidently told you I had it all together. But I was mistaken. I went to the Howard School Building to get my new business license for ICS not realizing that I hadn't closed my previous business. This presented a problem because I had to pay the taxes for that business prior to getting the license for ICS. Anago carried the insurance for R&R so that was another hurdle that I had to clear. I was lost when it came to General Liability insurance, and I never had to deal with Workman's Comp so that wasn't even on my radar. With my business license and ICS registered as a sole proprietor, I was almost equipped with all the tools to getting my life and business on track... or so I thought.

By this time, I had gotten my license, which was an ordeal. I still didn't understand how your license could get revoked for committing a crime. It would seem that one has nothing to do with the other. The first car I purchased was a 2004 Buick Century. However, I knew that the proposals and solicitations I would be submitting would require a different type of car, so I went to a "tote the note" lot and purchased a 2004 blue Astro van. A wise man once said, 'do what you can with what you have where you are.', so I embodied that quote. I printed some business cards on Vistaprint and would spend my days going from door to door rebuilding my company's brand. I'm thankful that I had a big contract that had stuck with me throughout my entrepreneurial career. As an early entrepreneur I had a little leverage. But I didn't want to put all of my eggs in one basket. Getting new customers was the only thing I focused on at that time. The traditional, door to door method wasn't as feasible in 2013. I thought to myself that there had to be a better way. How were all the other janitorial companies successful?

After six months of filling odd end jobs I realized that I was underbidding and that all money wasn't good money. I also didn't fully understand how to bid. At the time, I was simply looking at jobs and quoting generic prices hoping to get my name out there. I called these types of jobs "suicide jobs." Who wouldn't accept quality work for pennies on the dollar? Companies would jump at the opportunity to have me work for them and even ask if I could complete the work the same day. I later found that the reason for this was because my prices were too sweet. The deals I offered were unfair to me and my business. I immediately realized that I needed a mentor in the industry. Someone who had been where I was and done the things I wanted to do. I went to a couple of black businessmen in the community in hopes that they would be eager to help me. I was wrong. It's unfortunate when you realize that most of the people you think would help you are usually the ones that won't. A big part of the reason some African Americans have regressed or are stagnant is because of the fear of competition and the jealousy others feel when they see someone succeed. To think that as black people we have to go outside of our community to find the information we need for success because we are afraid of our neighbor getting ahead of us is shameful. I would name the people who didn't help me, but I can't... that's not the purpose of this book. After realizing all of this I started to look for organizations that would help budding entrepreneurs with practical advice.

I discovered SCORE and the Nashville Incubation Center when I was in prison. I never frequented these, but they were resources that were readily available to me. I even looked into using the EC. I then met the President of J.U.M.P., Sharon Hurt. We were introduced through a mutual friend. Using these connections and the little money I had I managed to get a small office on Jefferson Street at the Frierson Center. I bartered services for the office space and paid a minimal fee. Mrs. Sharon was a loving kind woman who I deem an angel. In my time of need she vowed to help me, and she followed through on that promise. After spending time with her we eventually became friends. She helped me learn about minority certifications and their benefits. She also helped me through the GODBE certification process. This opened many doors including the

Airport DBE certifications, the TSMSDC certification, and my fire and odor restoration technician certification. But the main point that I want you to remember here is that the certifications didn't make your company; it was your ability to leverage and maximize opportunities.

Even with the certifications I still needed a mentor. The certifications did grant me opportunities to meet with other industry leaders, but I still needed someone who could offer me guidance. After a lot of searching and inquiring I finally found a mentor, Daniel Brimer, who owns XCI Building Services. I met Daniel through an area manager with Premier Building Services. Daniel is younger than me but has more intelligence and wisdom than you would think. I thank God that He placed him in my life. Daniel has taught and continues to teach me about business. Words cannot truly express just how thankful I am for our friendship. But it didn't stop there, God blessed me with another angel named Pat Conroy who is the CFO of a national company. Pat is a father figure to me. He keeps me on the straight and narrow, makes sure my business is operating properly and gives me the hard truth even when it hurts. He is someone that I am very grateful for...not only for his honesty, but also for his friendship. You often didn't experience the joy of having people around you that have your back through the ups and downs when you're an entrepreneur, but I'd truly been blessed. Of course, I've had my brother, Josh Mundy, who rode for me, but we serviced two different industries. Darren has become like my family. His wife Carla and my cousin Chantae are like best friends, so we are very close. You could say our meeting was kind of like destiny. We currently do business with one another, utilizing each of our individual strengths to help complement our companies. Darren has also helped me pull in some big accounts which helped my company a lot.

Around this time, old Blue's motor blew up and I had to find another way to service accounts. I went to another tote-the-note lot and purchased a red 2003 Chevy Venture. It was almost destiny in a way since ICS's color scheme is red and gold. The Chevy Venture ran for a while and eventually quit on me. I then finally decided to buy my first real van. A 2002 Ford F-250. I was excited because I could finally wrap my vehicle and look like a 'big boy' company. The motto "Fake it 'til you make it" was definitely something I lived by. I learned that sometimes you have to improvise until you get to your destination. Especially when your dreams and ambitions are larger than life.

CHAPTER 12

Hard Work Pays Off

Society and social media teaches us that wishing on a star would get you what you want. That almost like a magic trick, success and notoriety would appear with a simple 'abracadabra,' but that couldn't be further from the truth. Success requires faith, patience, persistence, and hard work. When you set a goal for yourself, sometimes, it's so far-fetched that at it the ideation of it, it seems impossible to achieve. I was just seeking to survive and provide for my family. I never thought that Imperial (ICS) would rise to the heights that it has currently. I was single handedly running the company by myself. I had no employees... it was just me working 24/7/365 to make it happen. No matter the bumps in the road, I found a way to overcome them because what I wanted was more than where I was. Being a felon with tattoos covering your body, it's hard for people to believe in you because of the stereotypes and generalizations associated with 'our type.' There were so many late nights and early mornings.

Many people didn't know that I suffered from anxiety. There were times that I sat in my van after a job to try and regain composure. The type of person I am, I try to conceal the pain and sufferings that I am going through... I just try to push through. I guess that can be credited to my childhood. The idea of never letting someone see your weaknesses is something instilled in men from a very early age. The one company that took a chance on me was Advance Financial. The owners, Mike and Tina, gave me an opportunity to prove that my company was worthy of such a contract. In the entrepreneur field, we call these types 'early adopters.' They have always believed in me and given me more chances to prove myself than society deems necessary. It says a lot when a person or group of people are willing to see past the mistakes of your past even after society has written you off. Mike and Tina are more than business owners who gave me an opportunity. They are family who truly wants to see me succeed. I am blessed that they saw something in me and looked beyond the shell to see my passion. This is where it started. I grew with this company from nineteen stores to nearly ninety stores and counting in all three regions of Tennessee. This catapulted me to another level of business and gave me the fuel I needed to grow my company.

"I was blessed to have Advance Financial..."

There were so many naysayers who doubted that a man like me could become successful. It's hard for people to see beyond lapses in judgement and their own perceptions of what success looks like. We were taught that 'success' came in seven figures, fame, and tailored suits, so a man with a felony and a body covered in tattoos from North Nashville definitely doesn't fit that image; however, true success is found in shattering molds and overcoming societal standards. We have to learn to define our own success and become our own fans. If we didn't believe in ourselves then how can we fault anyone else for not believing also? We find more fuel in the idea of fame than in the passion of our purpose.

I've had the money before. I was an entrepreneur before it was a trend, in a way. Buying low, selling high. Customer service. Business management. Operations. Strategy. All of the tools necessary to run a business, I learned as a hustler. I took what I knew and implemented it in a legal entity. The whole time I was in prison, I wrestled with the idea of being broke when I got out and how I would make it back to the top. I wasn't willing to sacrifice the time with my family, but I knew that there was a way and it would be hard. The motto 'hard work pays off' became a way of life, and I refused to stop until I got what I wanted.

I was blessed to have Advance Financial, Metro General, HCA, and Capital View Project as concurrent clients. This yielded more for my company than I could have imagined. It was almost overwhelming but refreshing... a conundrum of sorts. So what did I do? I balled. Every luxury and self-prescribed fix that I wanted, I got. Not truly understanding that company money wasn't Robert's money. Stupid? Yes. Worth it? Maybe. Lesson learned? Definitely. We all have these ideas of what we would do when the money came

> **" As a business owner, you have to learn and know every facet of your company and operations.**

in... the items we would buy, the trips we would take, the ice we would rock, the designers we would drape ourselves in, the cars we would drive, the homes we would reside in, the bottles we would pop... the list goes on and on. No one tells us that ninety-eight percent of the things that we desire would depreciate, so a majority of our purchases are like throwing money in the trash.

They only add value to (insert blah) and not your bank account. Is it some form of self-validation filling voids deep within us caused by our desire to fit in society's mold? We use materialistic items to increase our value in the eyes of those around us without truly valuing ourselves beyond the tangible. Even in daydreams of things we would buy, we rarely think about the cost of doing business. They say all money ain't good money, but regardless Uncle Sam would want his piece of the pie. And that is a lesson that I had to learn the hard way. Spending company money on personal desires, Uncle Sam came for a visit in the form of a tax audit. I owed sixty-eight-thousand dollars, and they wanted their money immediately. I was blessed to be able to write the check, but the pain I felt was indescribable. This was my own doing. As a business owner, you have to learn and know every facet of your company and operations. From human resources to accounting, management to marketing, you MUST understand what is happening in your business at all times. You didn't have to master each department, but you should be versed in the subject. My lessons were all trial and error. Even after the

> **I've accomplished more as a business owner than I could have ever imagined.**

sixty-eight-thousand-dollar fiasco, Department of Labor and Tennessee's Department of Revenue reached out and needed a check. Little did I know, you couldn't write checks to people and not pay the taxes. SUTA, FUTA and FICA are all acronyms that I know now because I had to pay then. It STILL didn't stop there. I didn't know that having employees required you to have general liability and workers compensation insurance, I only thought you had to have general liability... so that was another check. Furthermore, having subcontractors required them to have up-to-date general liability, workers compensation, and a business license. There is an audit at the end of the year that checks for this and if not, there is a penalty. So, of course, I had to write another check. When dealing in human resources, I-9s and W-4s are required as a part of the hiring process. Even in an at-will state, when you move to terminate a person without proper documentation explaining why, that employee is able to file unemployment. If filed enough, it would raise your rate exponentially and require... you guessed it... another check. Add to this the overhead of running your business, maintenance, payroll, utilities, and a wide array of other expenses, you truly learn that it does cost to be the boss. Educating yourself on business is a must.

Hard work does pay off. I've accomplished more as a business owner than I could have ever imagined. I am thankful to God and very humbled because I was able to experience success and failure at the same time. I learned my lessons and know what not to do the next time around. I am also able to share my downfalls with others in hopes of prohibiting them from making the same mistakes that I made. I think I haven't made it near the tip of my mountain and that my greatest success is yet to come. I have no college degree and no formal training, yet I've run and operated a million-dollar company and started RCS Holdings, a real estate management and investment firm, Impact Youth Outreach, a non-profit combating youth crime with positive relationships and mentoring and partnered with my friends to form TWC Enterprises (theLAB Nashville) and Music City Photo Booth. I've won Nashville's 40 under 40 and Black Chamber's Rising Star, been named one of Nashville's most influential African Americans and was a consumer advocate on Capitol Hill where I sat on a panel in front of Financial Services Committee. I've been featured and mentioned in many publications for my accomplishments.

The journey to the top is never easy. We struggle to find landings to rest, grips to assist in the climb, endurance to keep us climbing, and persistence so we don't quit when it gets too tough. Everyone's mountain isn't the same, but we all have our own journey. Keep climbing, even when you are tired. They say the view is beautiful from the top. You'll slip. You'll wonder if it's really worth it. You'll want to quit. You'll kill many milestones one day and won't progress an inch the next. But it's worth it. Every trial. Every obstacle. Every tear. Every doubt. Every failure. Keep climbing. Keep pushing. Keep going. Embrace your journey. Maybe, just maybe, the journey is about unbecoming everything you've become to make room for who you were destined to be. It wasn't perfect or pretty... it was turbulent and honest... it's not fiction or embellished. This was the story of how losing everything gave me the perfect slate to build my future on. My then made me tough enough to endure the journey back to my now.

THOUGHTS

OF

A KING

A CALL TO ARMS

written while incarcerated at Forrest City Federal Penitentiary

The Truth War

I am going to speak figuratively for a moment. I come to you today feeling fed up, disgusted and saddened by the horror that we as a people are experiencing. There is nothing that hurts more than being at war and your soldiers are not ready for battle. As a matter of fact, they do not even know how to fight. And already, the enemy is standing on the hill giving the order to attack. To make things even worse, we cannot even see the weapons being formed against us. Hosea 4:6—My people are destroyed from lack of knowledge.

In today's society, there is a war waging. The war I speak of is not physical, but mental and spiritual. Immoral precepts against moral precepts. The soldiers that I speak of are our black brothers in our communities, and in our prison systems. They are subjecting themselves by a misconception of how a real man is supposed to function in society. We are enticed and lead astray by distorted gangster stereotypes and glorified lifestyles flooding today's multimedia platforms with misleading realities that can make success appear easy and fast—all of which cultivates greed and compulsive behaviors and entitled attitudes in our youth and culture. I believe this ultimately impairs our focus and spending power.

While many are indulging in tangible materialism, the most cherished asset that is key to our survival slips from our grasp. This asset I speak of is knowledge, which is the most powerful weapon we need, and one in which we must have to fight. Knowledge truly is power.

While we play a game that the enemy creates, designed specifically for failure, thinking that we can win, we are losing our lives, families, communities, our dignity and self-identification. Proverbs 14:12—There is a way which seem right unto man, but the end thereof are the ways of death. We have black brothers walking around with negligent attitudes, degrading one another because they have no substance that is of value in themselves. This is due to lack of education and lacking the necessary father figures to guide them. As a result, they substitute what is lacking with characteristics that are immoral, degenerate and unprofitable. Proverbs 16:18—Pride goes before destruction and a haughty spirit before a proud fall.

How can life that is meant to be primitive become so much of an enigma. This disease of malice from one another is impartial and prevalent. So much that you have the CDC doing statistics on the murder rate of black individuals. The statistics I wish to quote are both daunting and pessimistic. Unless we lay hold and adhere to change, this vicious cycle could be very much so perpetual at the rate its progressing.

We as black men must continue to be proficient at our goals of waking one another up. As individuals we must remain fervent to what is requisite for our young brothers to be converted back to real men, putting away all strife, and subjugated mind states. We must contend to rise from the depths and eradicate old behaviors and mentalities. We must become a new man that is profitable, spiritual, responsible, loving, intelligent, and equipped to be a man of integrity—the man we are all destined to be. Because we were not meant to be sons of perdition, we were made to be sons of God.

Amen.

--Robert Sherrill

The Rise. The Fall. The Redemption.

Most of the time, when we are in the dark and have been for a while, we struggle to see the light at the end of the tunnel or the saving grace. We know light and grace exists...we know it can't stay dark forever and that tough times don't last always... we just can't imagine when peace will arrive. Depending on what caused the darkness, most of us don't feel worthy of being saved. The decisions we made to get here, the many signs we saw to turn back that we ignored and the desire to continue on in a way that pleased us without thought of the consequences. When you are living life on a high, you aren't able to truly see what is going on. You have rose colored glasses. Everything is good until it isn't. And when it isn't, we wallow in the dark spot...making ourselves comfortable in the rut because the thought of recovering from such a fall and lapse as the one we just experienced is overwhelming and the action seems impossible. We embrace the rise, despise the fall and discount the redemptive possibilities. But each stage builds our character and shapes us for the greater good and our divine purpose... whether we know it or not.

The rise

The trip to the peak is one of the greatest feelings in the world. We think we are invincible because everything is going right. We lose sight of the world around us because we are caught up in the mirror we are standing in front of. The thought of falling or losing it all is non-existent and when it does cross our mind, we push it to the back or justify our actions with 'just one more time' or 'this is the last time' knowing that we will continue to chase the high that we are experiencing. We're focused, or so we think, on here and now, with little regard for the now and later. Our plans or thoughts don't last past the moment of self-perceived success or hype.

In history, we learn about the rise of many great empires, but the greatest ones also have a greater story of how they fell or declined. The fall isn't from lack of power, but the settling into comfort. Being pacified with complacency, becoming undisciplined and thinking that the seat at the top is guaranteed only by reaching it often ruins, ruined or will ruin any empire… including yours. We are so blinded by achieving the goal that we don't consider the work required to stay at the top. Consistency is key and when it is missing, the decline starts to happen. The fall may be slow or it may be quick, but, without a doubt, it happens.

The fall

Every person experiences a low in life. A majority of the time, the fall is due to our own poor choices, bad decisions or inability to see past what is directly in front of us. It usually comes from the comfort of familiarity and a strong resistance for change or the desire to see those around us content without consideration of the effect that has on us, our performance and our desire to push on. Regardless, we all hit rock bottom after experiencing some kind of high. But the choice to stay there is what makes us uniquely different. It's easy to lay there and succumb to the pain, wallowing in the sadness of our new, temporary reality, but true strength is found in the rise. Proverbs 24:16 tells us that the righteous fall seven times, but he gets up again. It's not unsightly or shameful to fall, but you have to stand up after each time.

We lost focus of what was important and placed value on items, idols and people who had no true value in our life and ultimately, we lose control of the journey. The low always pales in comparison to the high and the deepest part of the valley always makes it seems like redemption is impossible. It is in these moments that we must remember the only way to lose is to remain down. Even when you feel like life is having its greatest boxing match with you, catch your breath, mend your wounds, get back up and set your stance. Going down and staying down is the only sure way to defeat. There is hope in the rise after the fall.

In crisis, your true character gets a chance to shine. When life is good, it is easy to smile, but when times are dark, finding that same passion, joy and kindness is a lot more difficult. Resilience in the face of failure is a trait that leaves us as we get older. As a child, we learn to do difficult things...to crawl, to walk, to talk, to read. We deal with losses and 'booboos' and bounce back better than before. It isn't until later, as we get older, that we pick up self-pitying. We pick up the idea that licking our wounds while whining will somehow produce a magic miracle that will fix itself. We know the work required to start the journey to the top again...we know the help that we need to ask and pray for...but we work against ourselves for a period of time. We grieve what we've lost and remain stuck in, what was to be, a short lived moment.

No fall is meant to harm us. Jeremiah 29:11 assures us of that very thing. But, we are a society focused on pain instead of motivated by hope. It is easier to accept defeat and blame circumstances for the hard times than it is to acknowledge the defeat, get back up and start again. But the latter is a requirement to keep moving. God didn't promise days without pain, laughter without sorrow or sun without rain, but He did promise strength for the day, comfort for the tears, and light for the way.

The redemption

Redemption is defined as the action of saving or being saved from sin, error or evil...the action of regaining or gaining possession of something in exchange for payment or clearing a debt. "Never say die" is a idiom that captures the power found in never giving up. We are all worthy of second chances...and in some cases third, fourth and fifth ones too. You have to believe that you are worthy to be redeemed...the idea of redemption requires the adoption of changed behaviors and new ways of life. Why redeem what is not changed? Through change, you show evolution. Through evolution, you show growth. Through growth, you add an attribute to your character that's needed to

MUGSHOT GALLERY

The Journey Back to Now   **151**

The Journey Back to Now

The Journey Back to Now

Made in the USA
Lexington, KY
28 March 2018